I0469392

Copyright © Colin Bentham 2016

All rights reserved. You may not copy, store, distribute, transmit, reproduce or otherwise make available this publication (or any part of it) in any form, or by any means (electronic, digital, optical, mechanical, photocopying, recording or otherwise), without the prior written permission of the author. Any person who does any unauthorized act in relation to this publication may be liable to criminal prosecution and civil claims for damages.

www.colin-bentham.com

Printed by CreateSpace, An Amazon.com Company

ISBN-13: 978-1530721573

ISBN-10: 1530721571

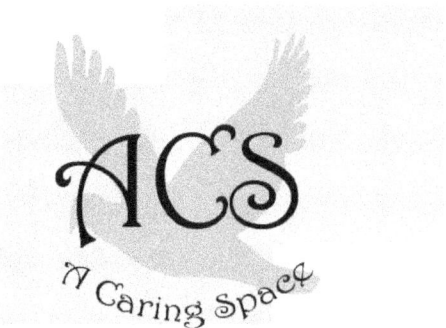

A Special thanks to A Caring Space at St Matthew's Community Halls. Who provide social activities for carers of people with learning and mental health difficulties. The brilliant team beta tested my work for the book during Art Therapy sessions.

Furness Creatives

Thanks also go to the guys at Furness Creatives for their support and encouragement in creating the artwork for this book.

Art is a mirror of the mind
and a reflection of the soul,

Our thoughts and dreams,
our imagination and wishes,

Brought forth from the realms
of possibilities and made real.

Colin Bentham

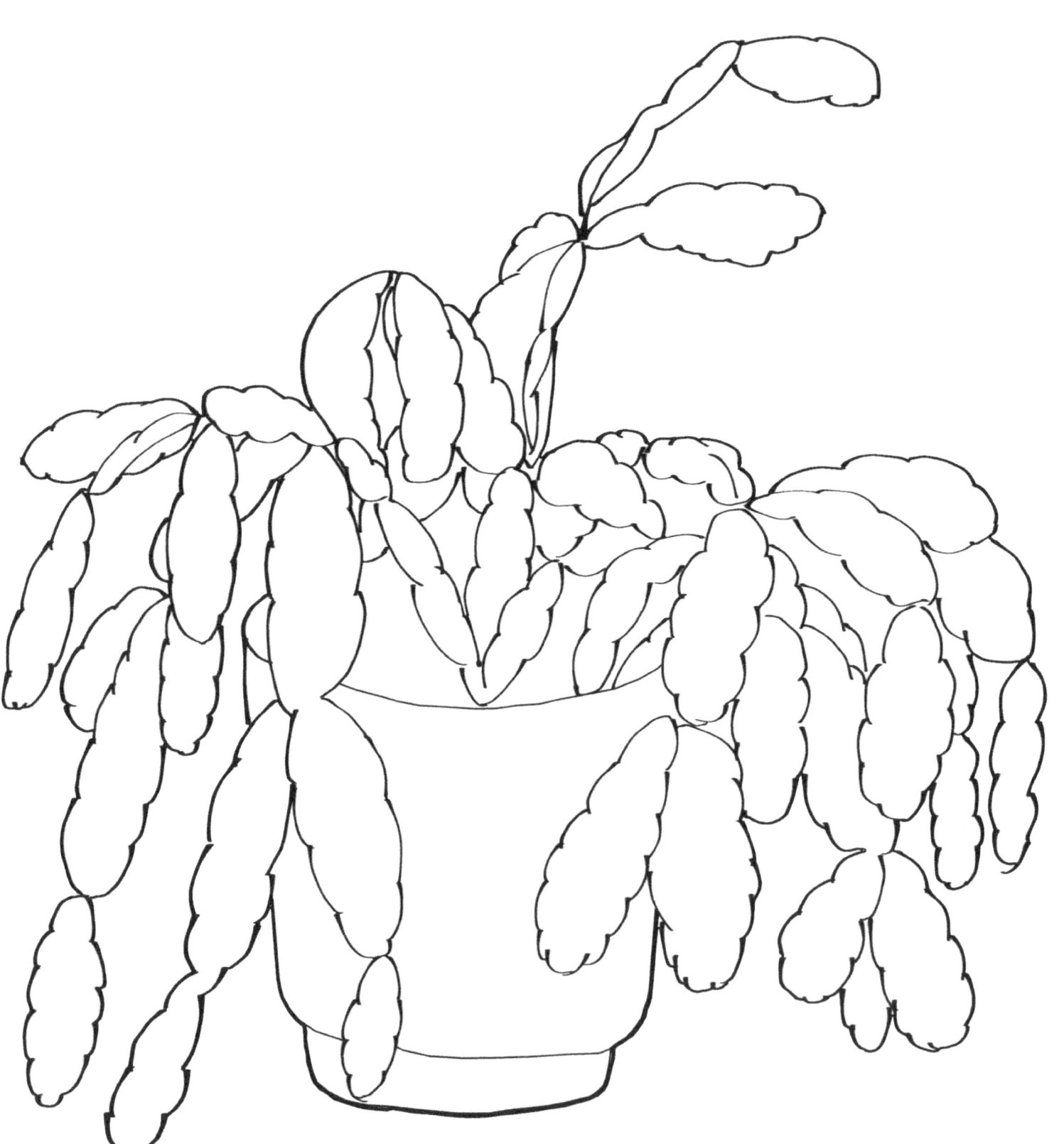

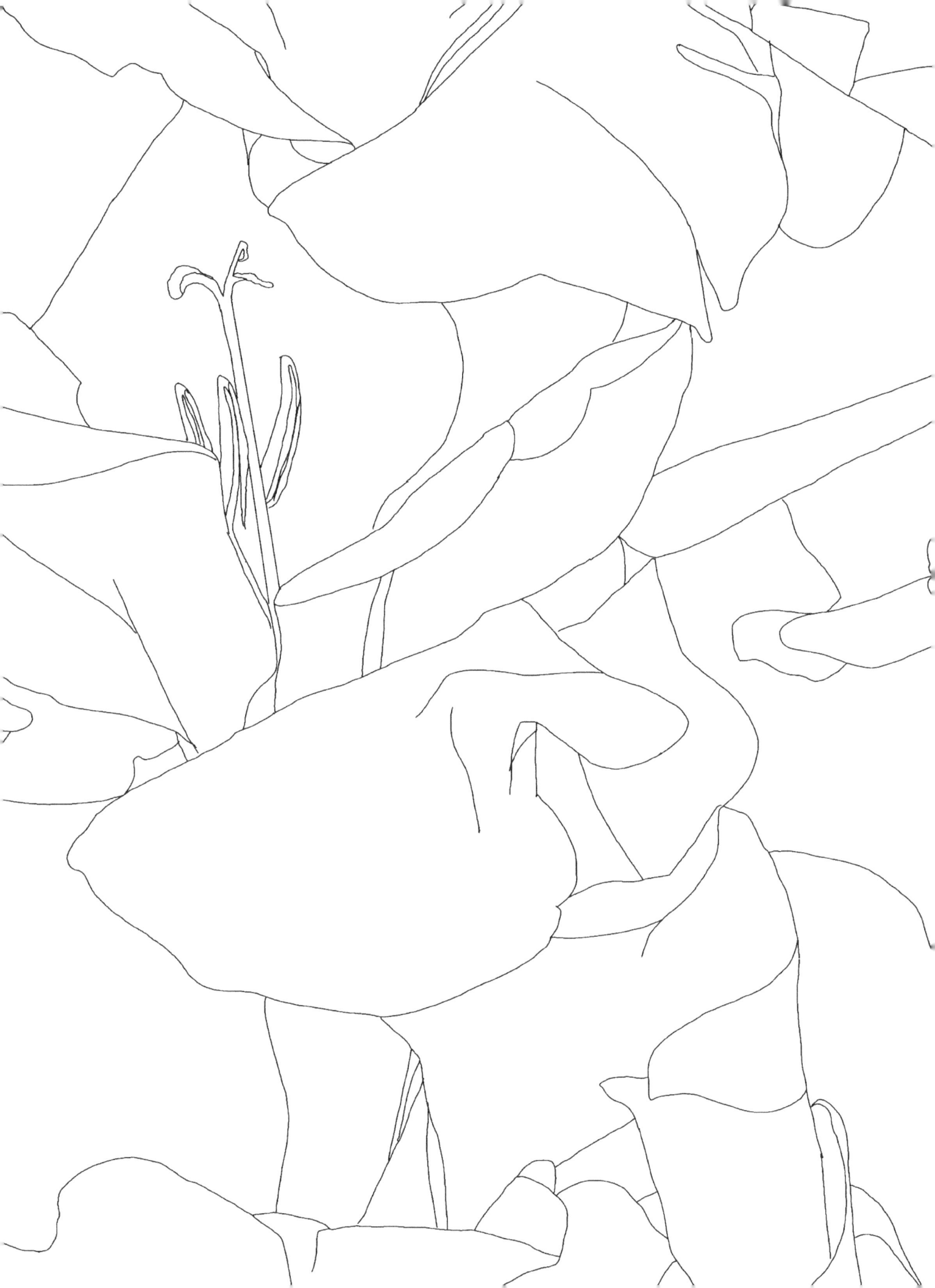

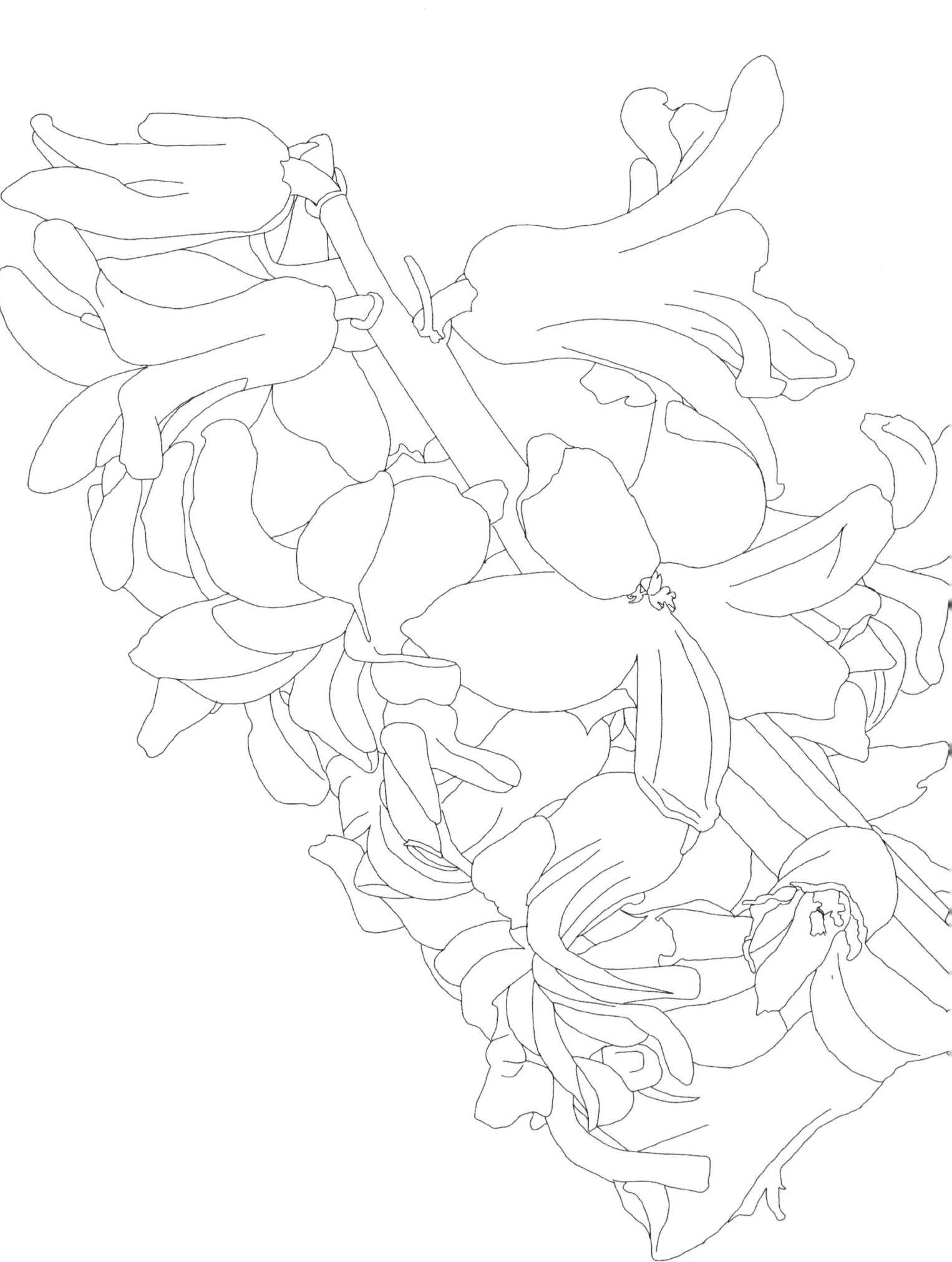

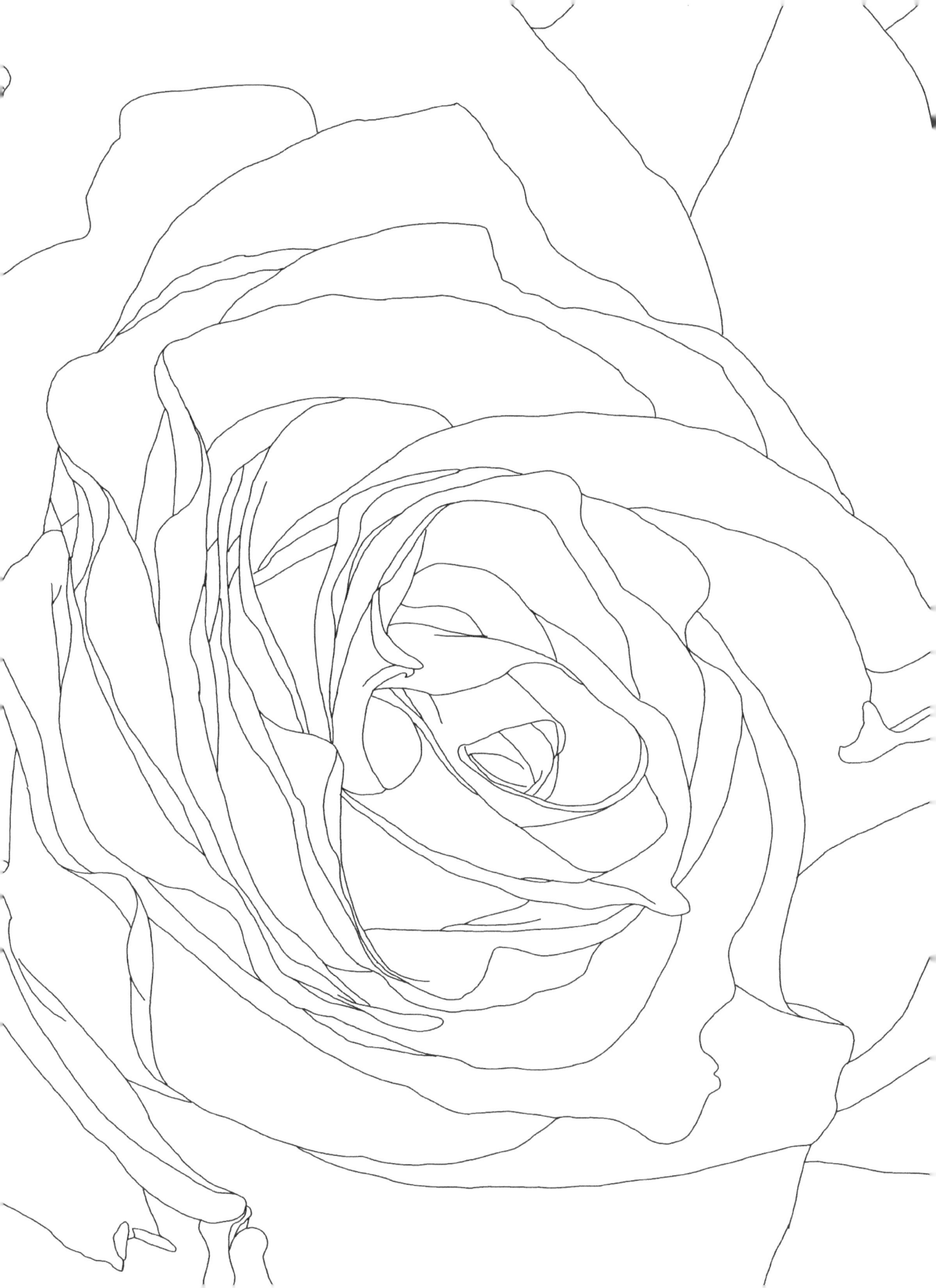

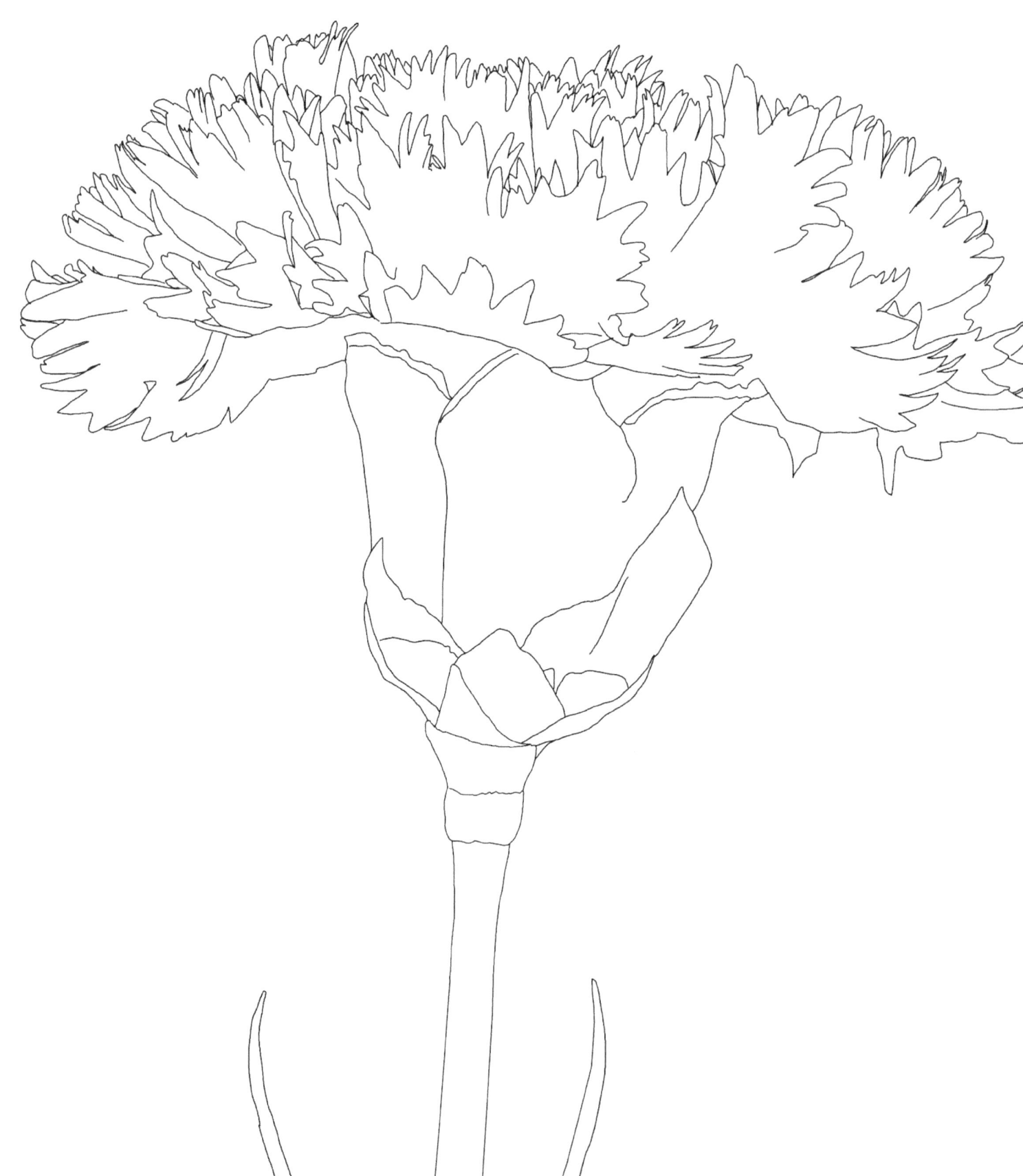

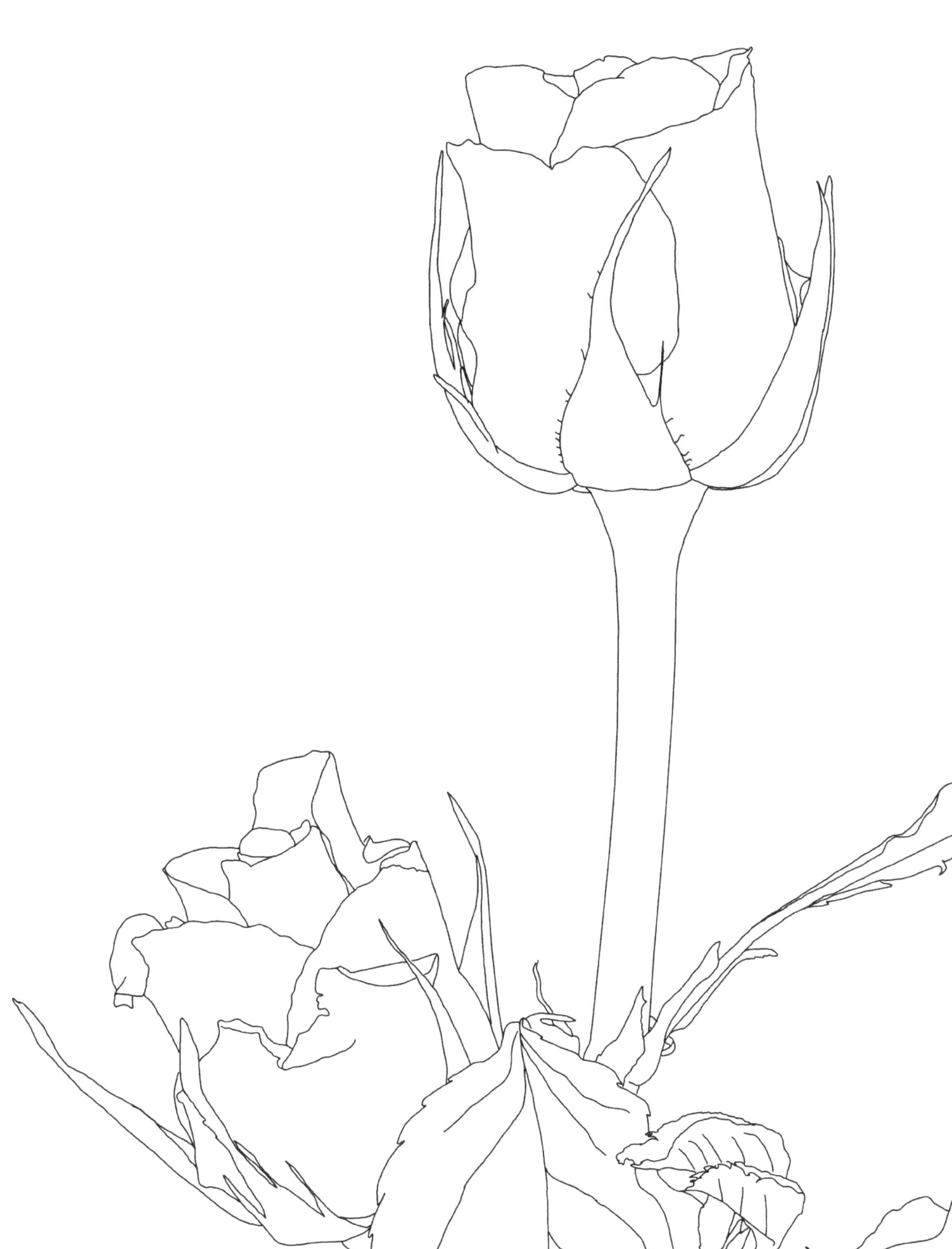

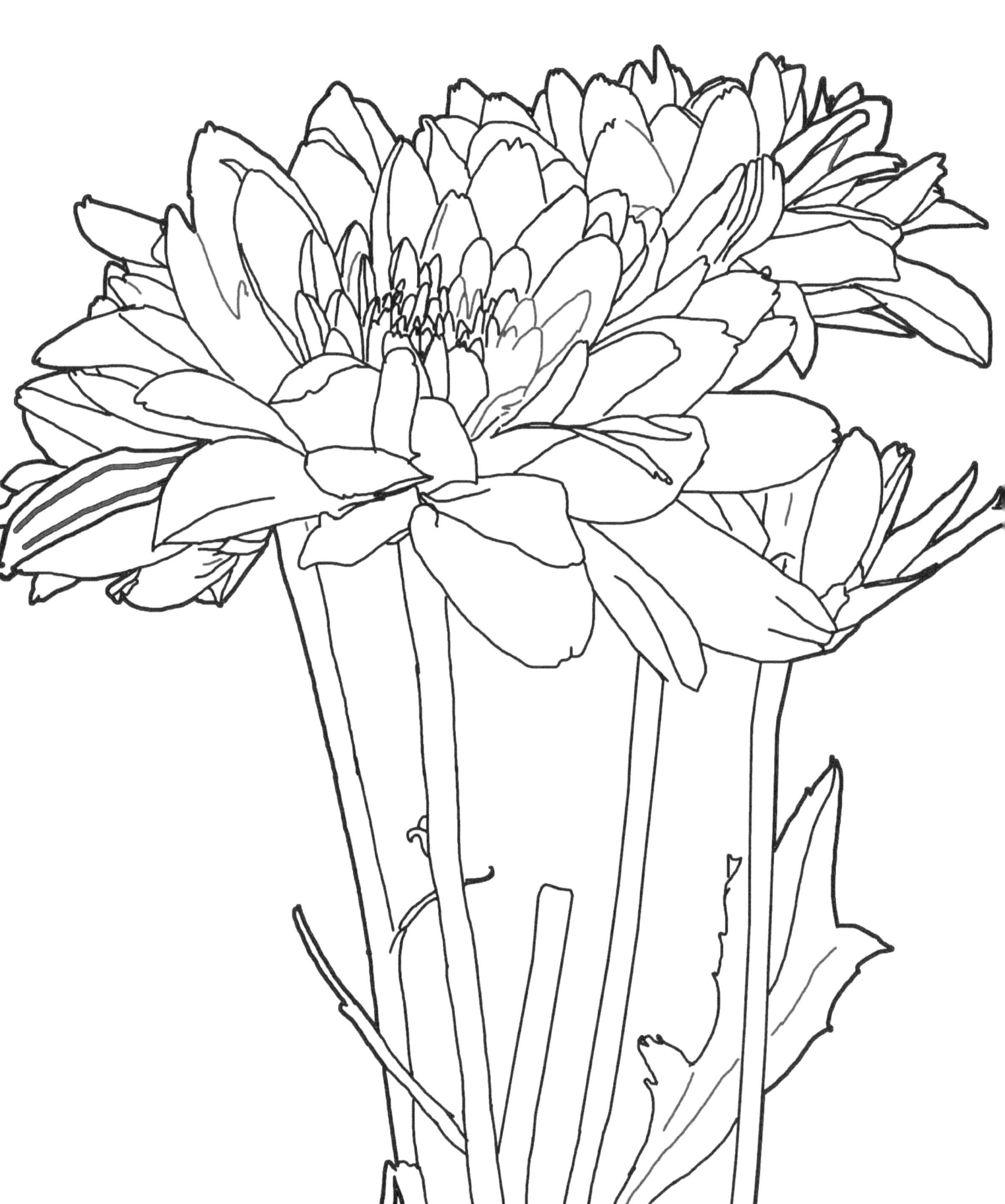

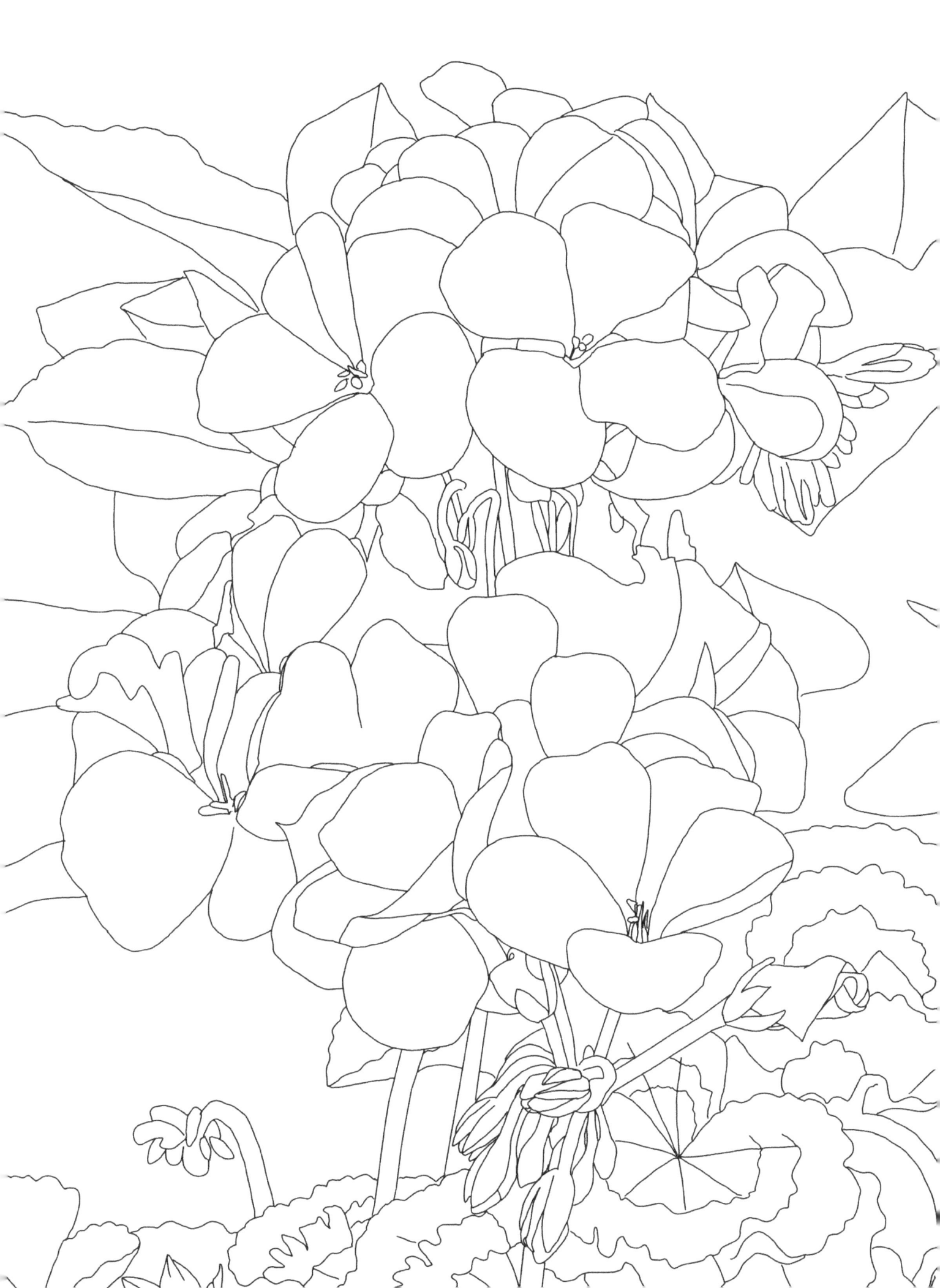

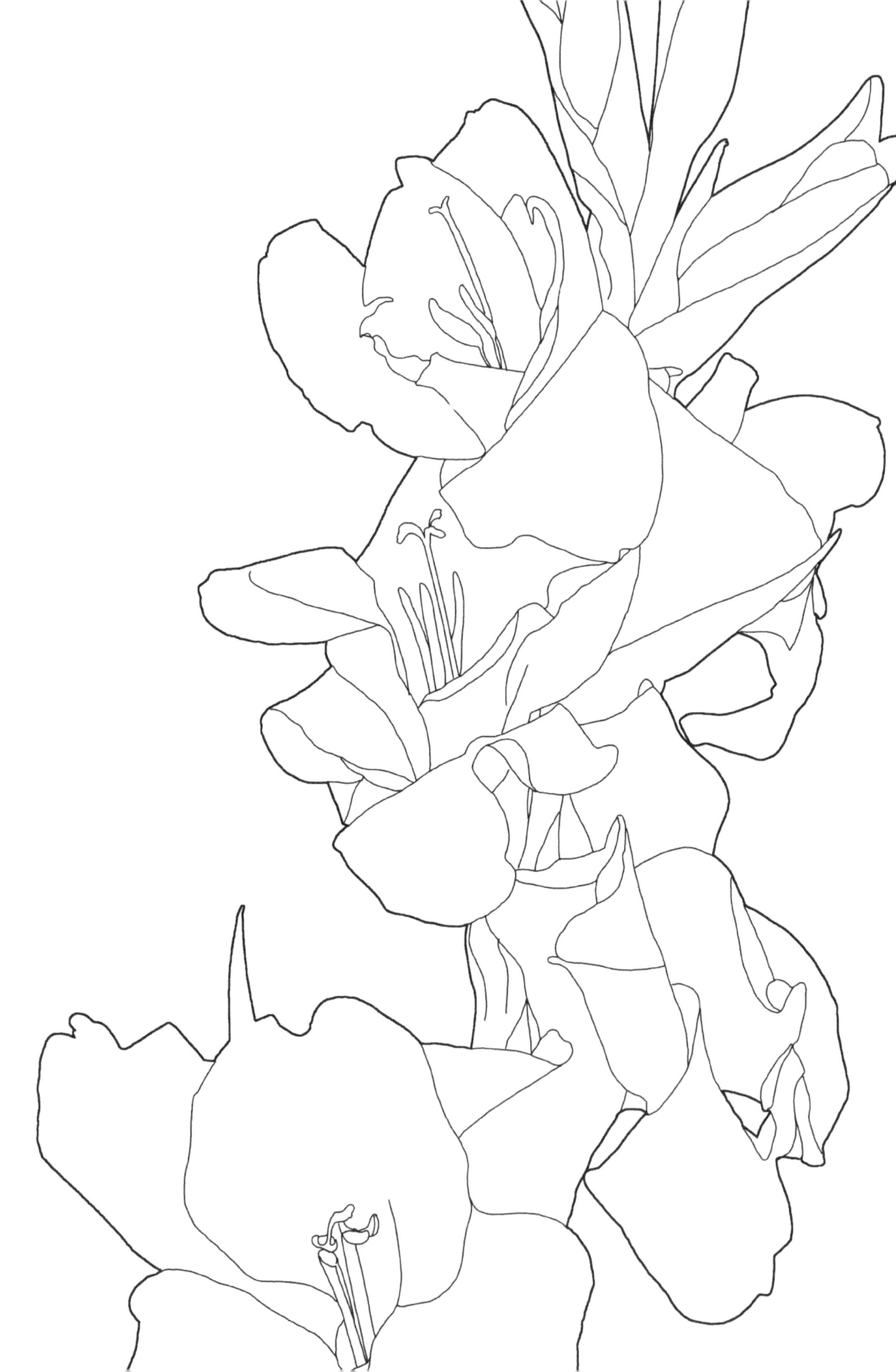

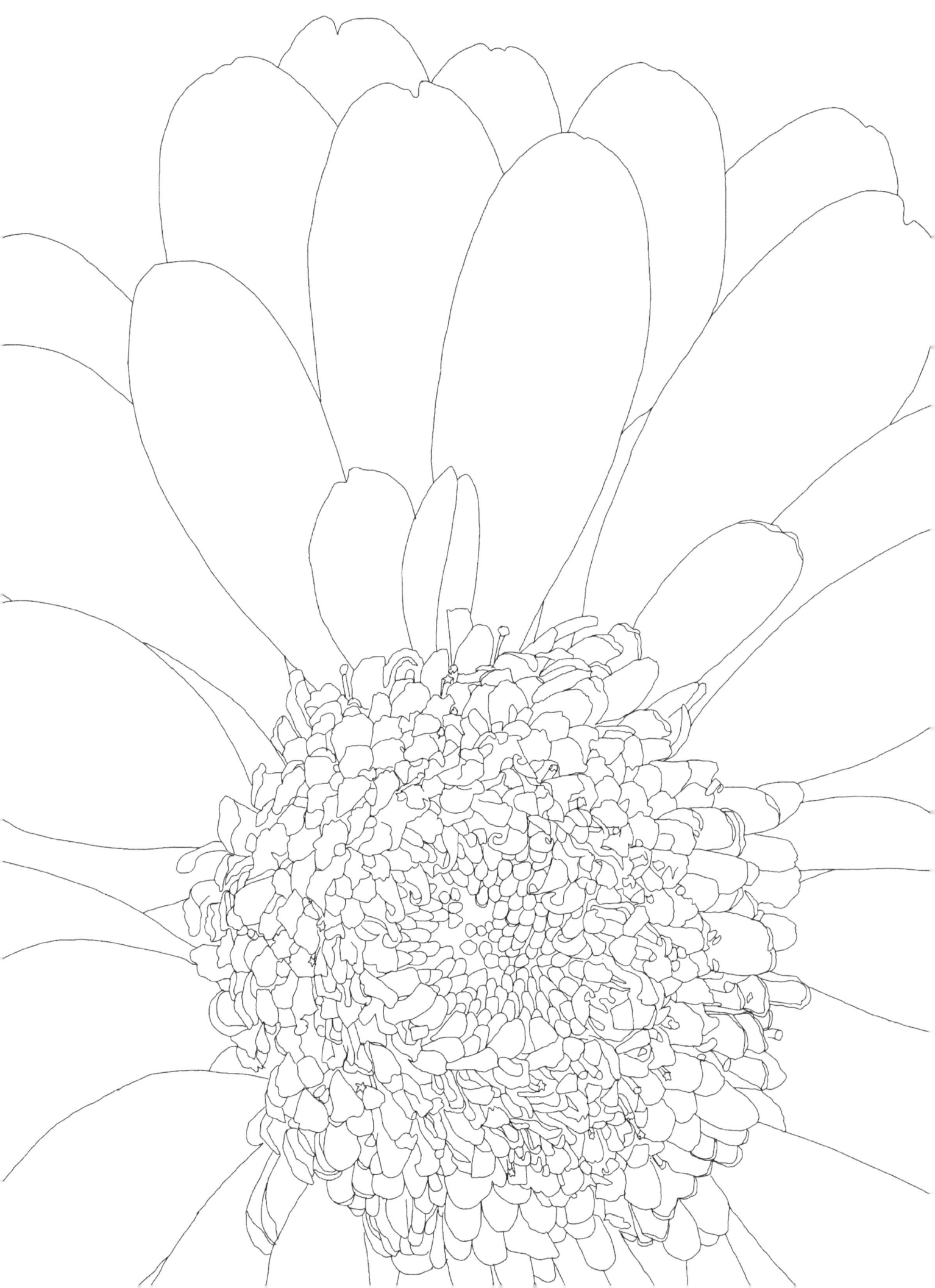

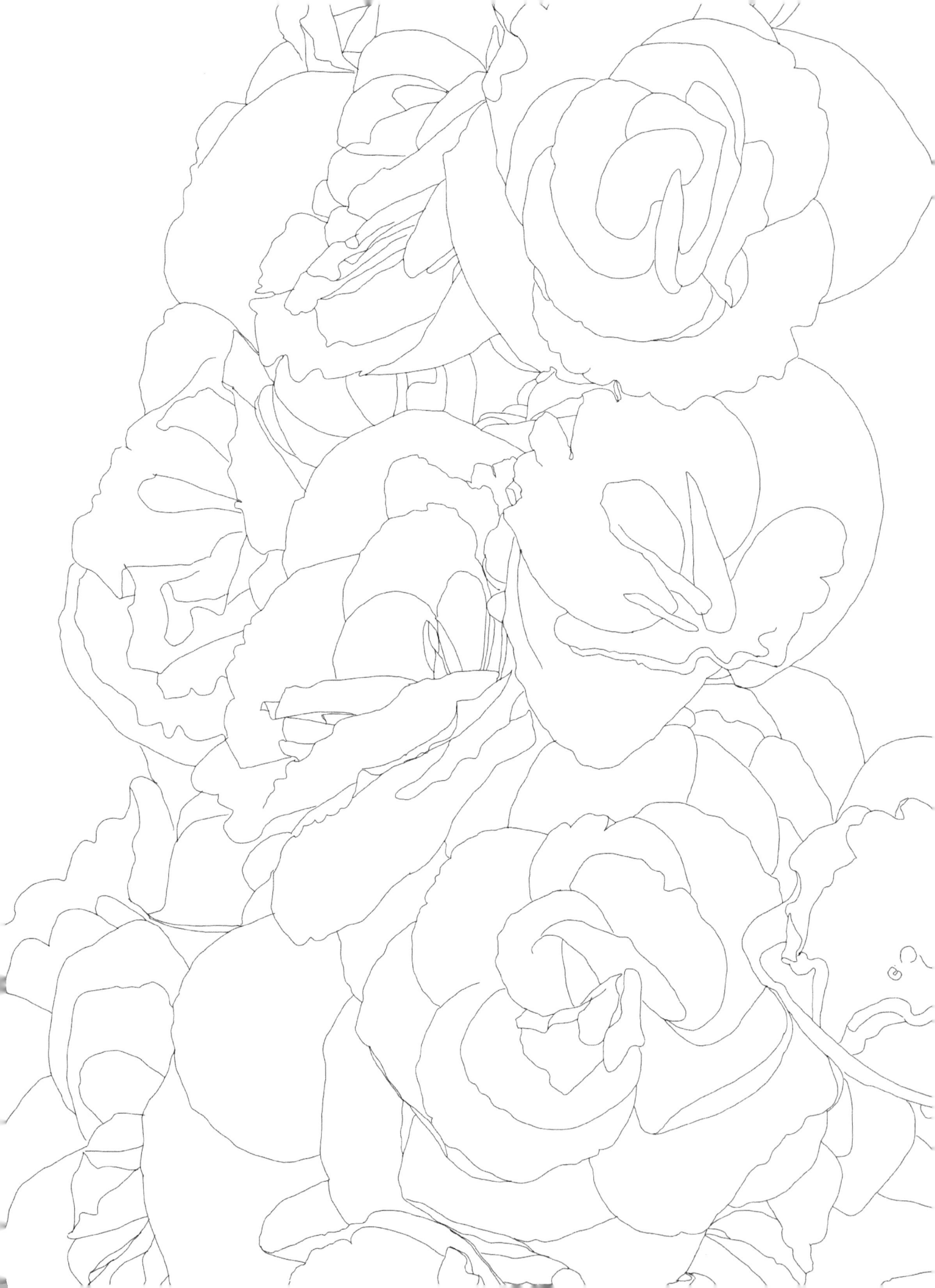

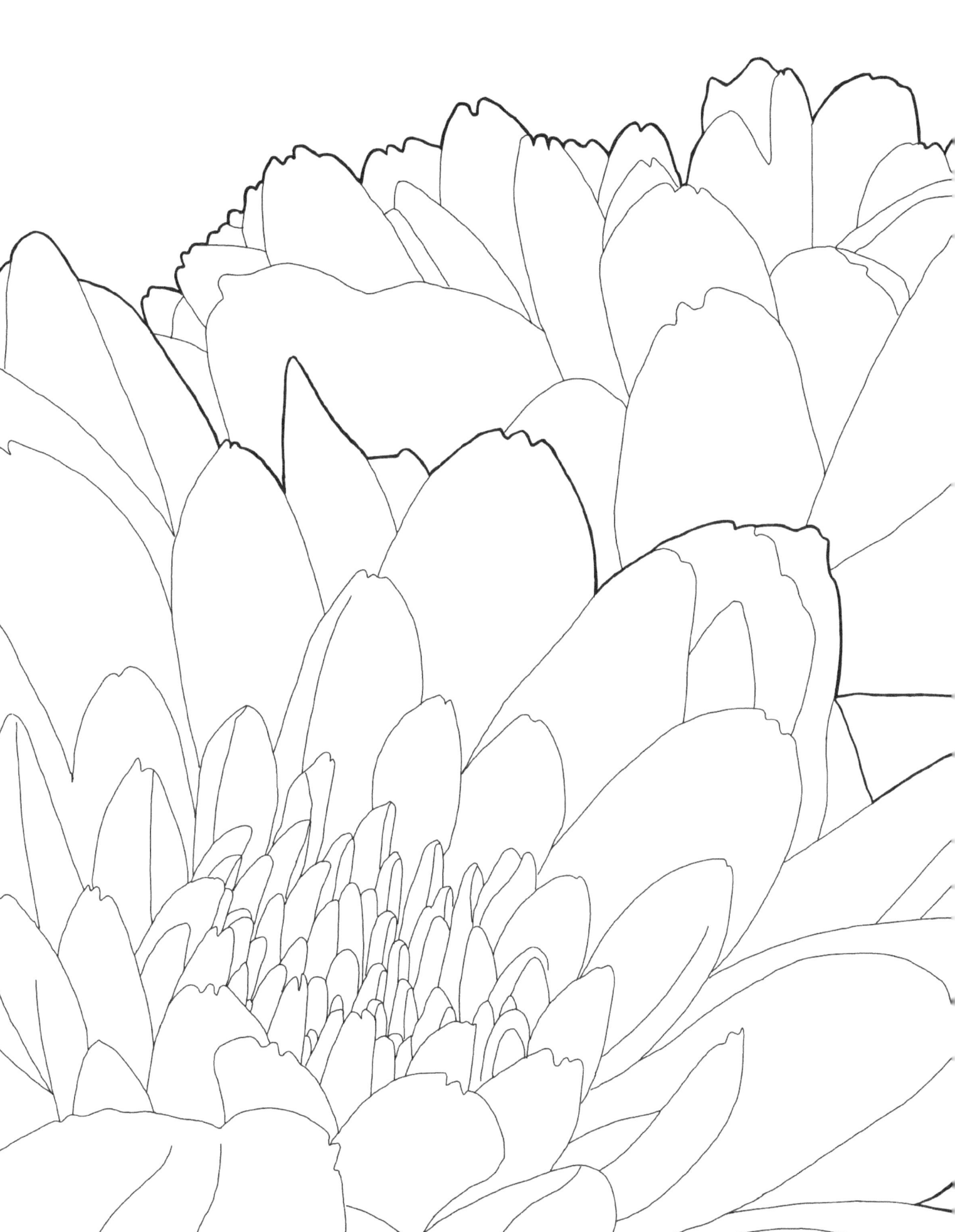

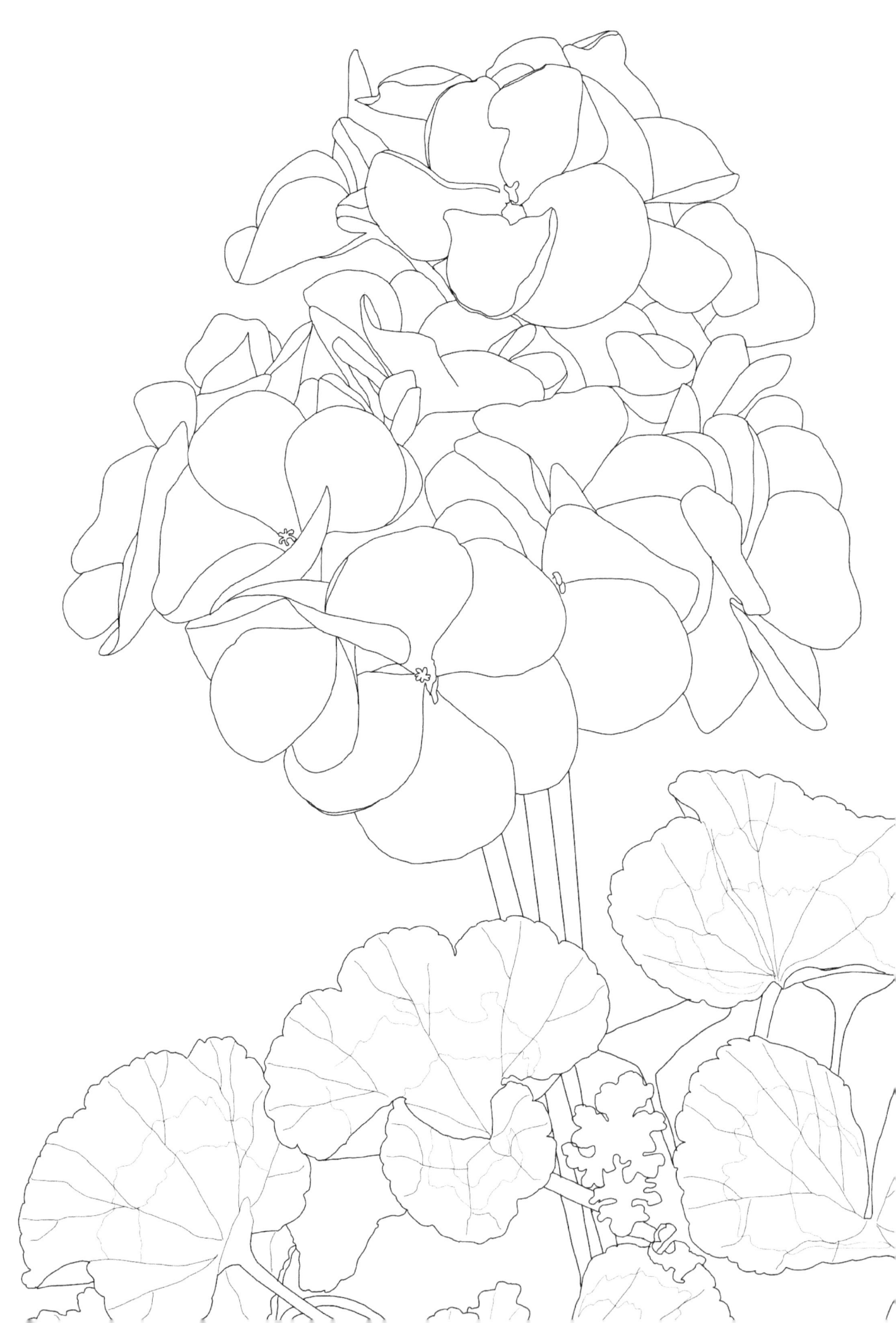

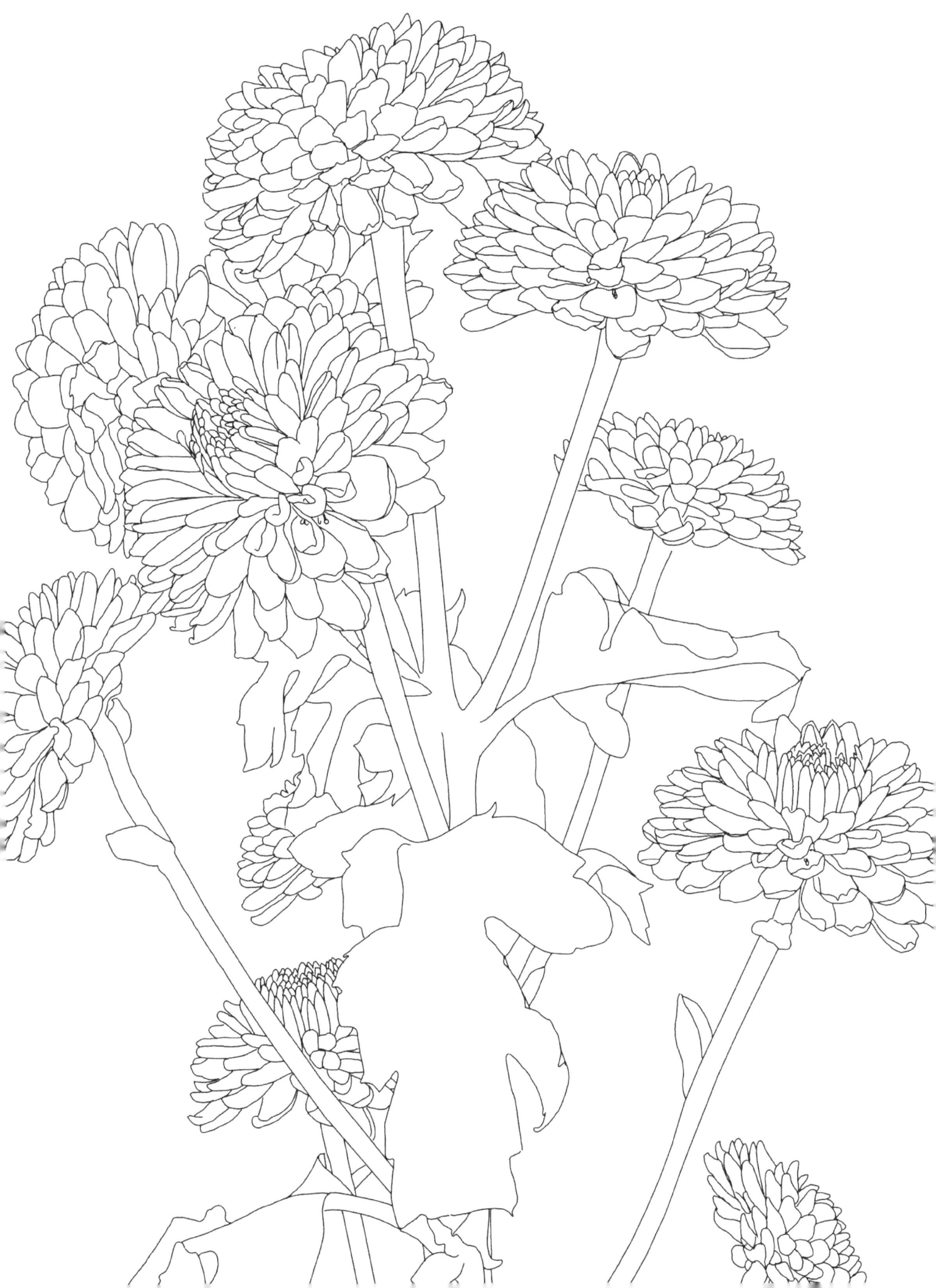

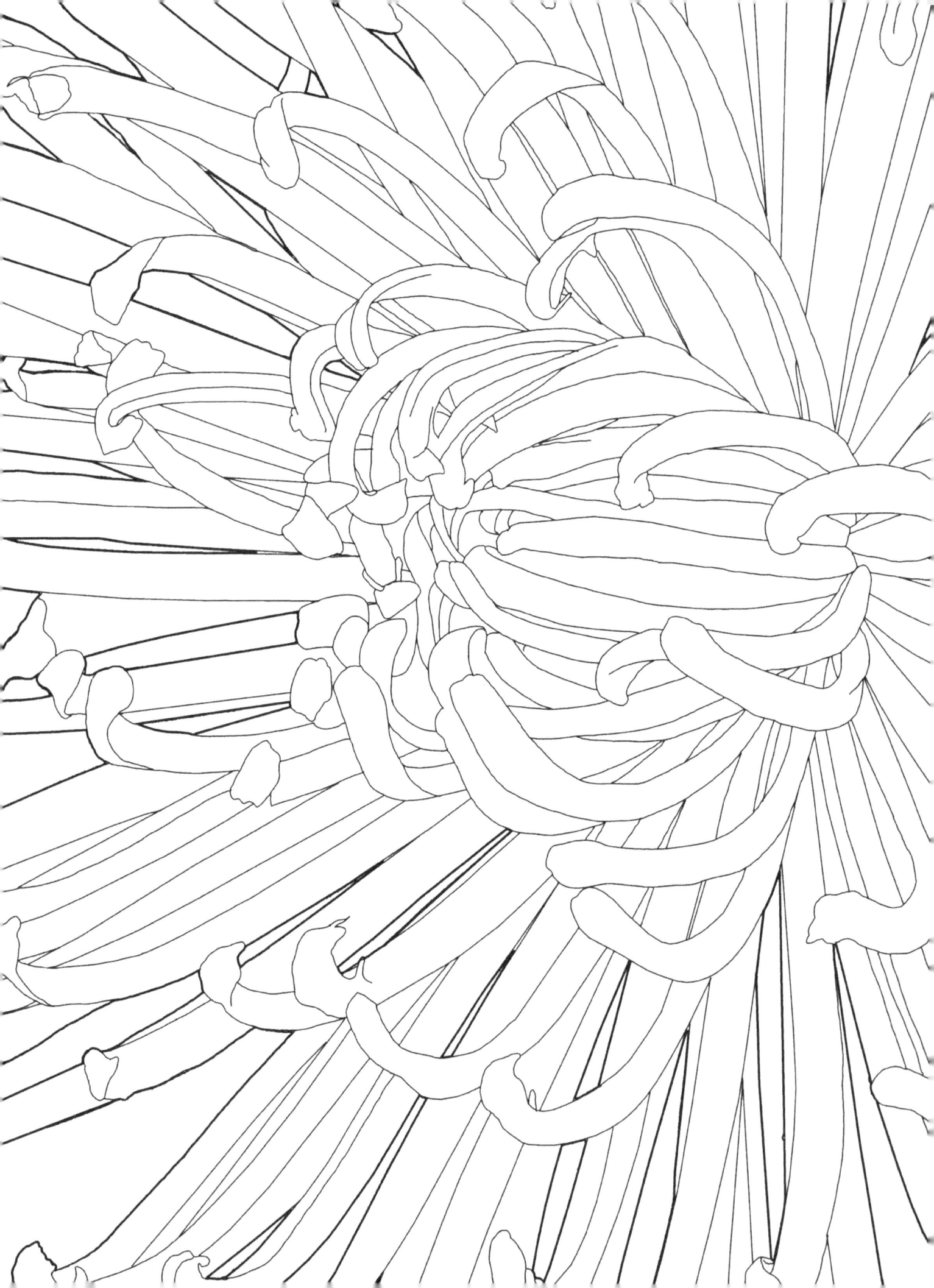

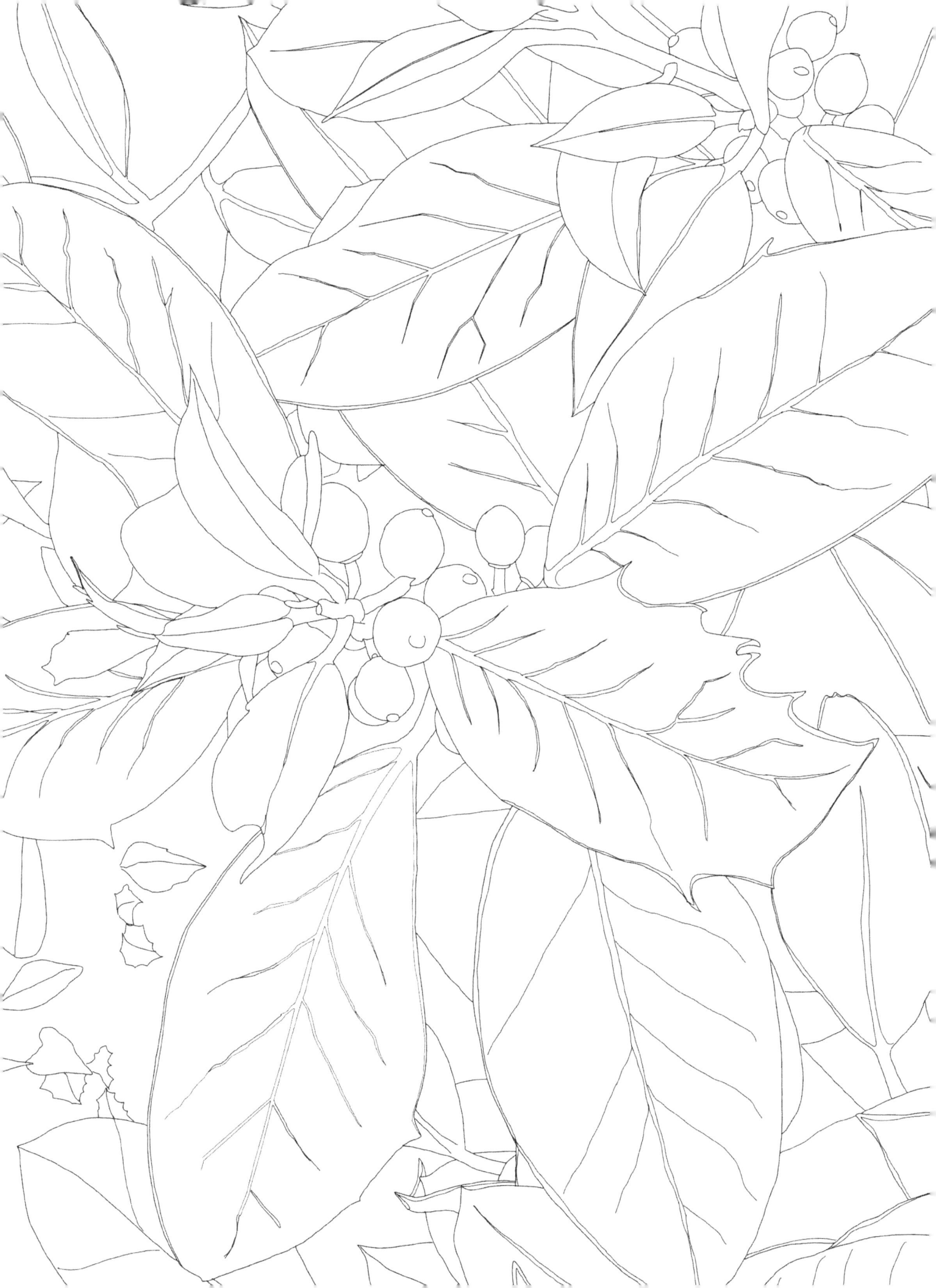

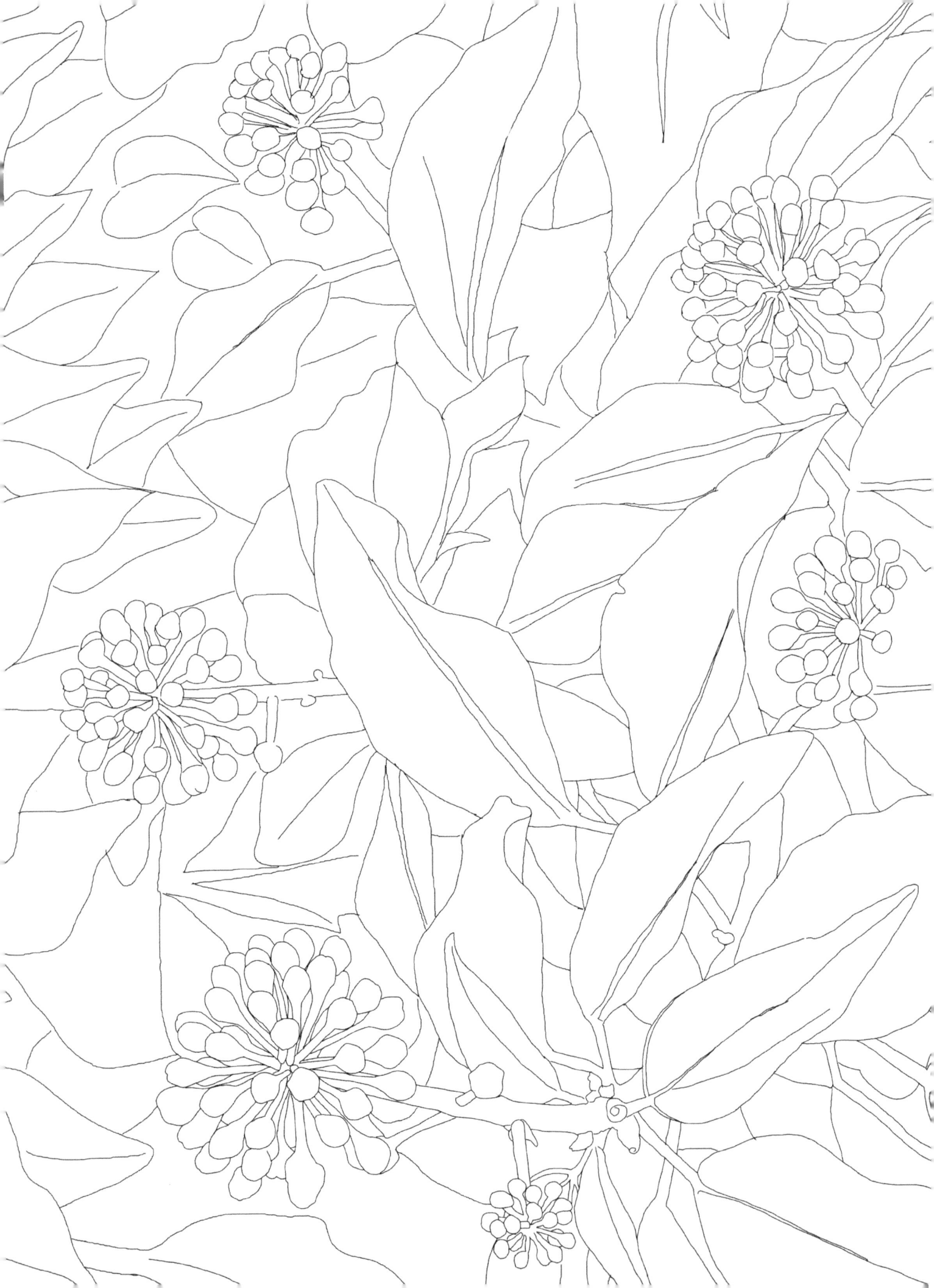

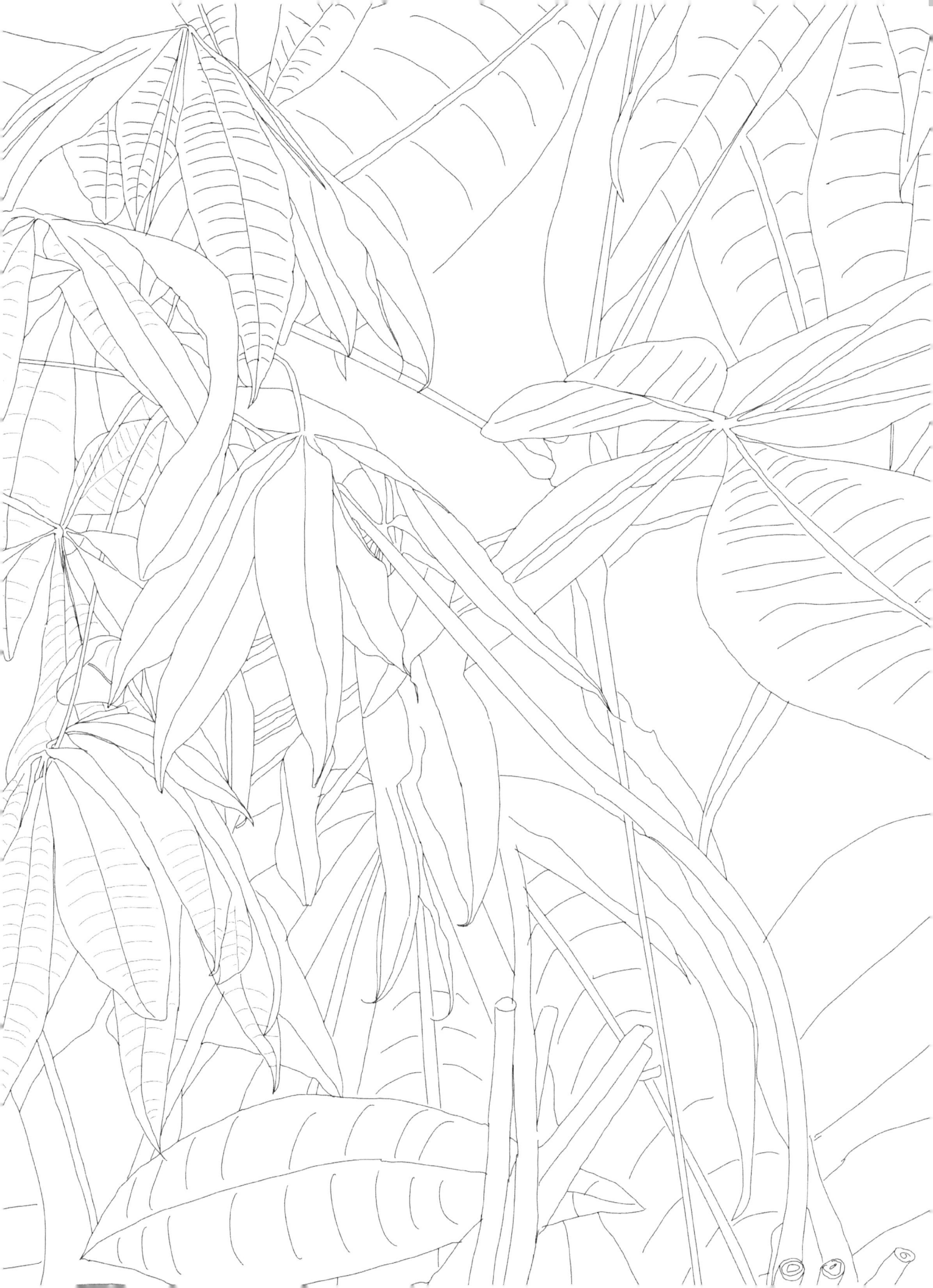

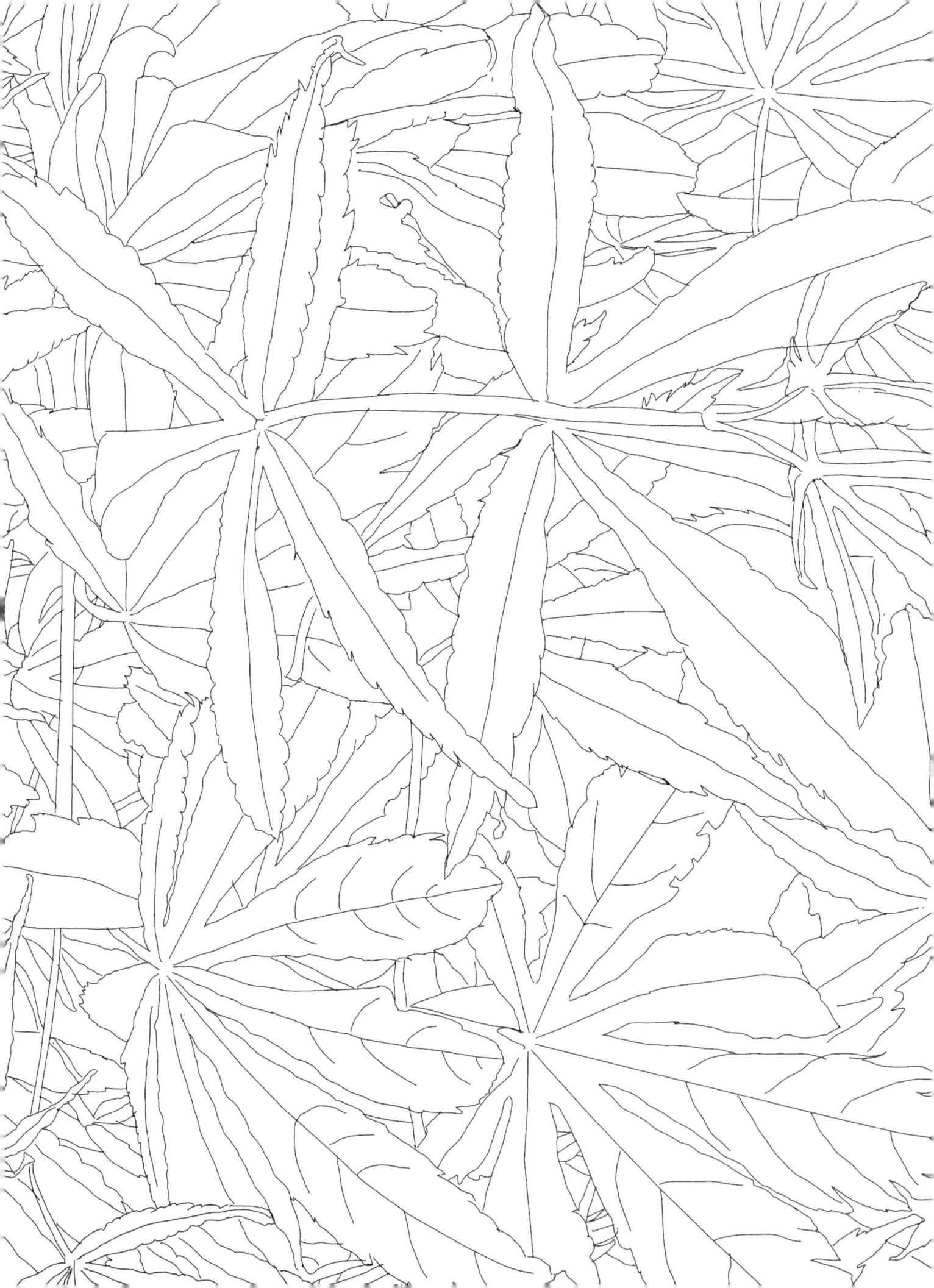

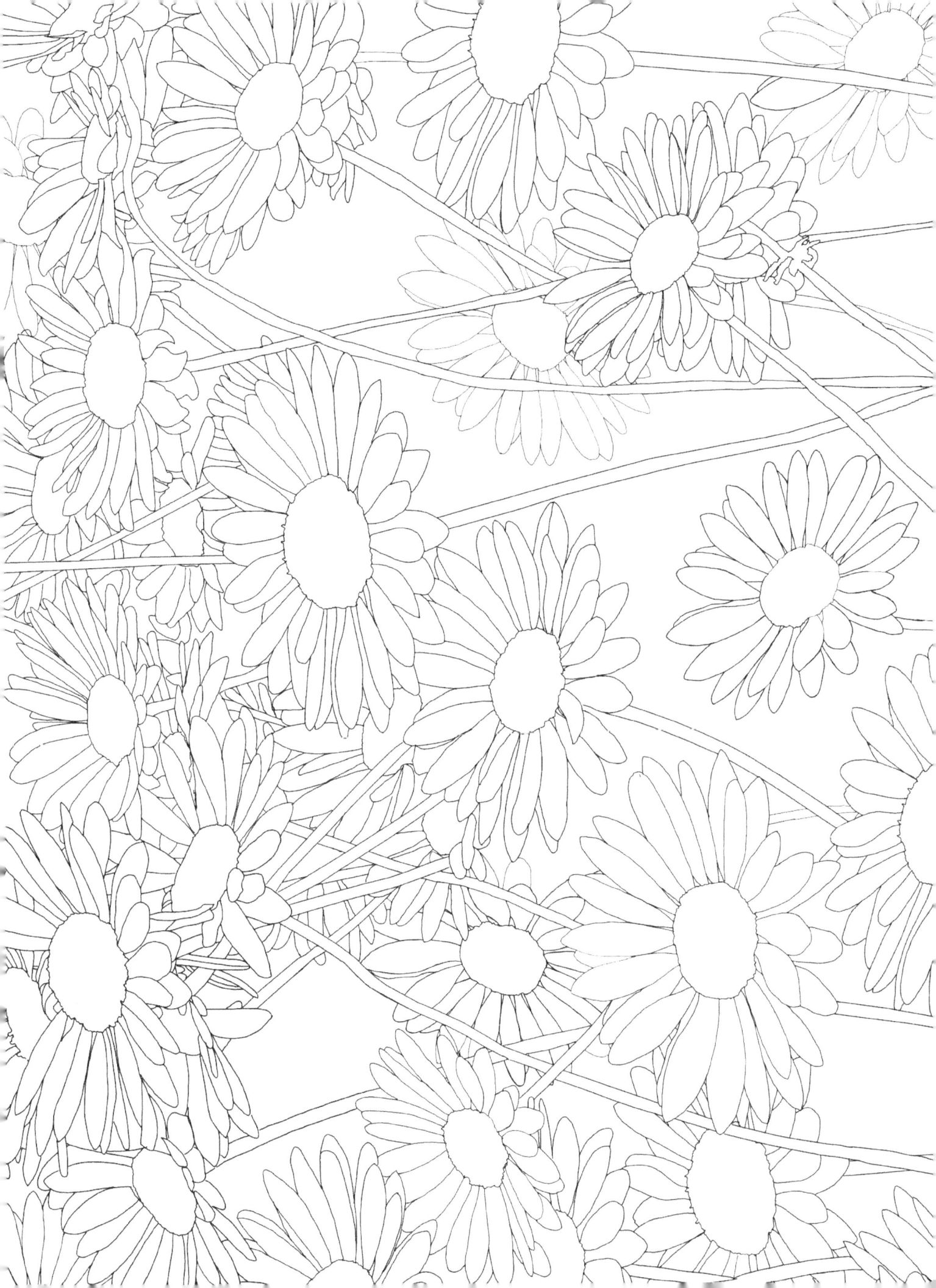

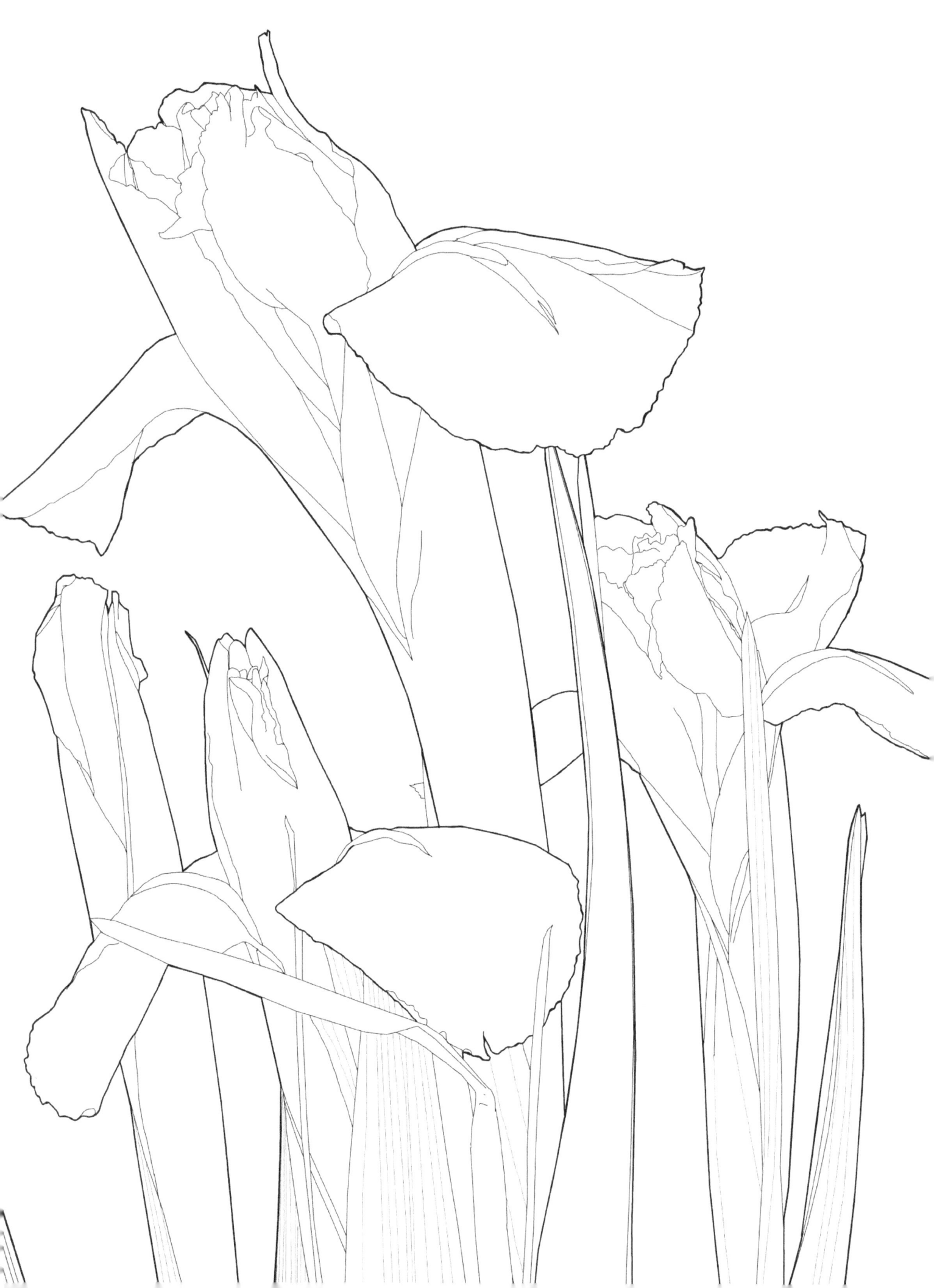

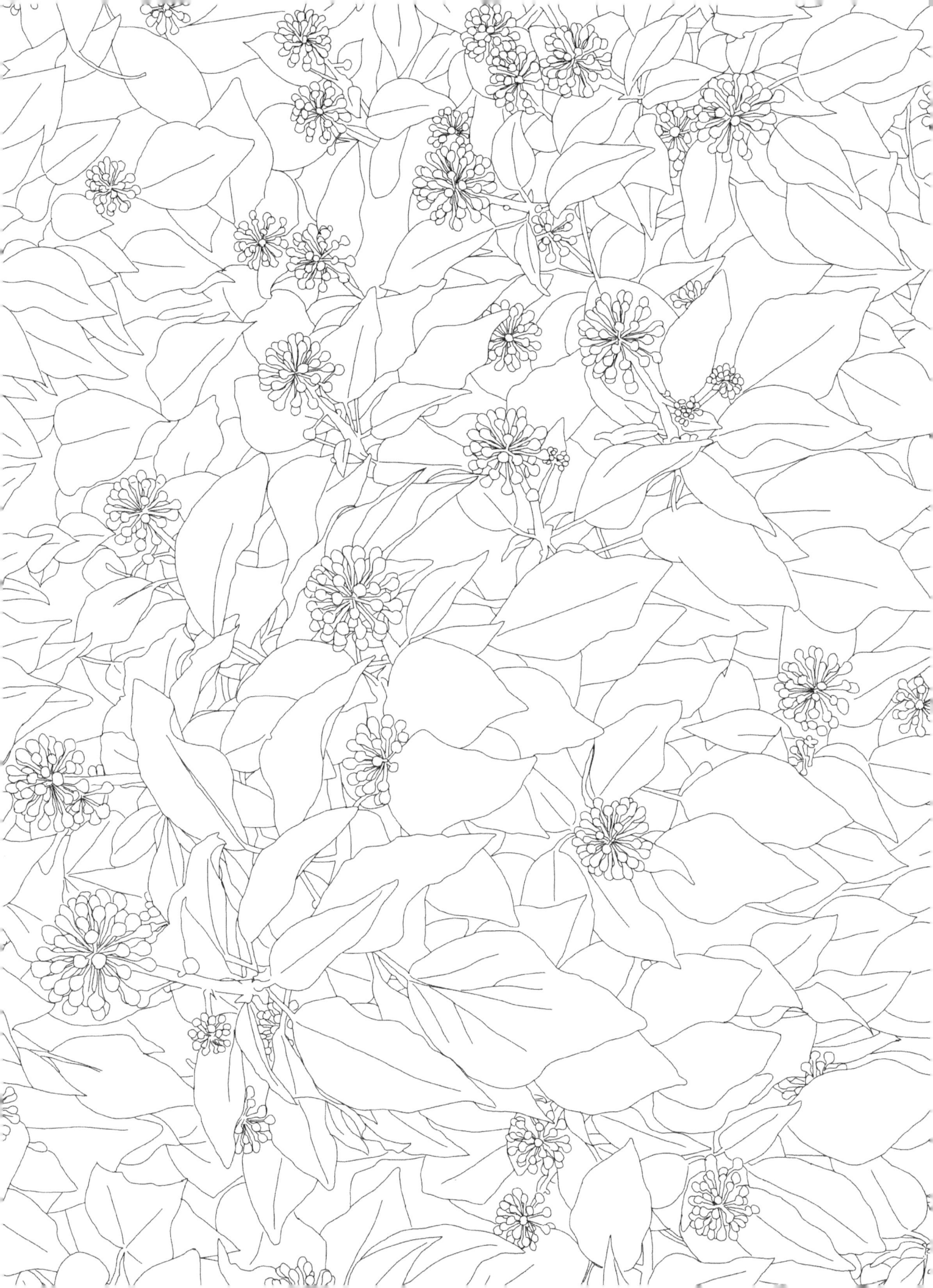

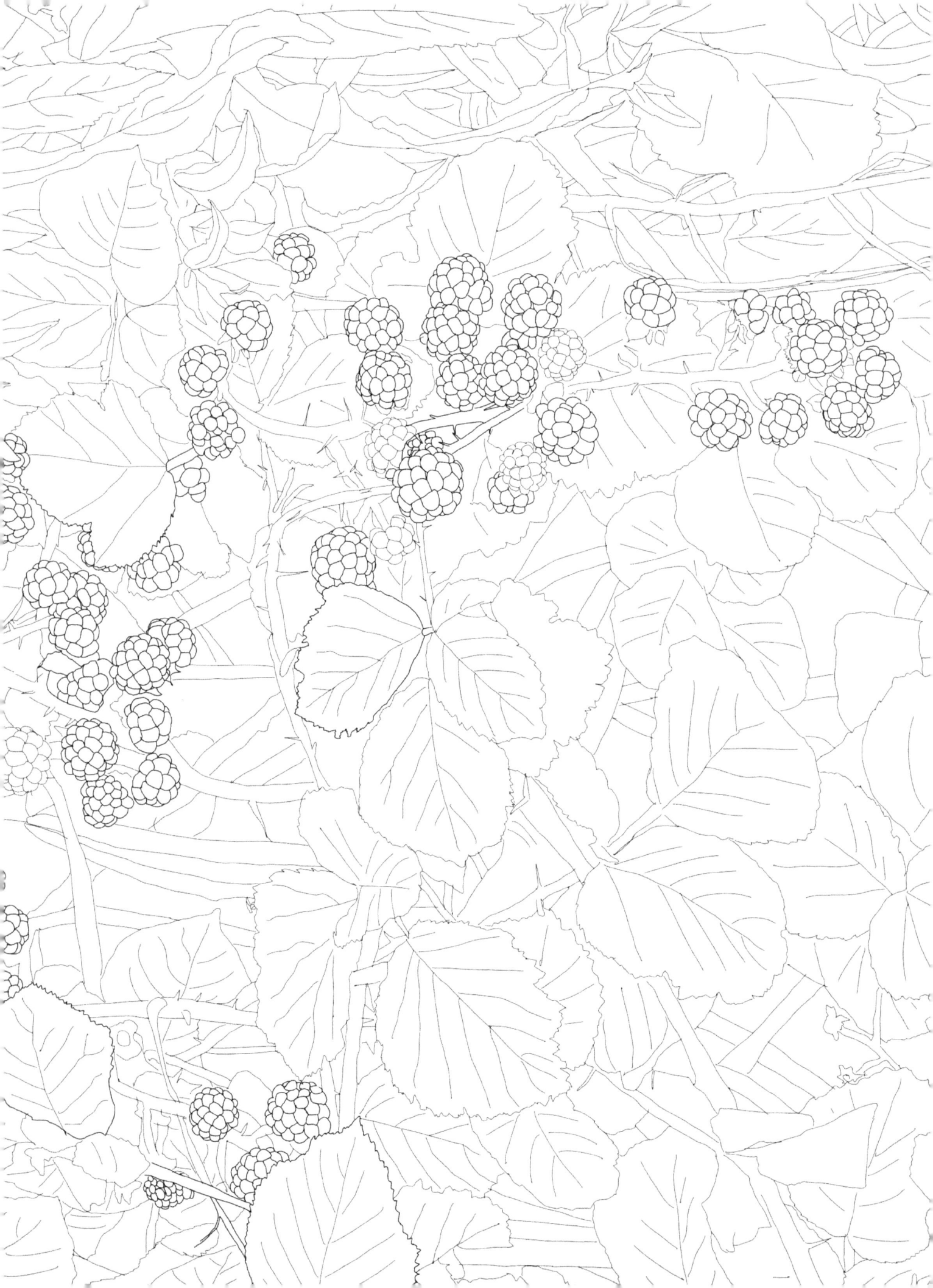

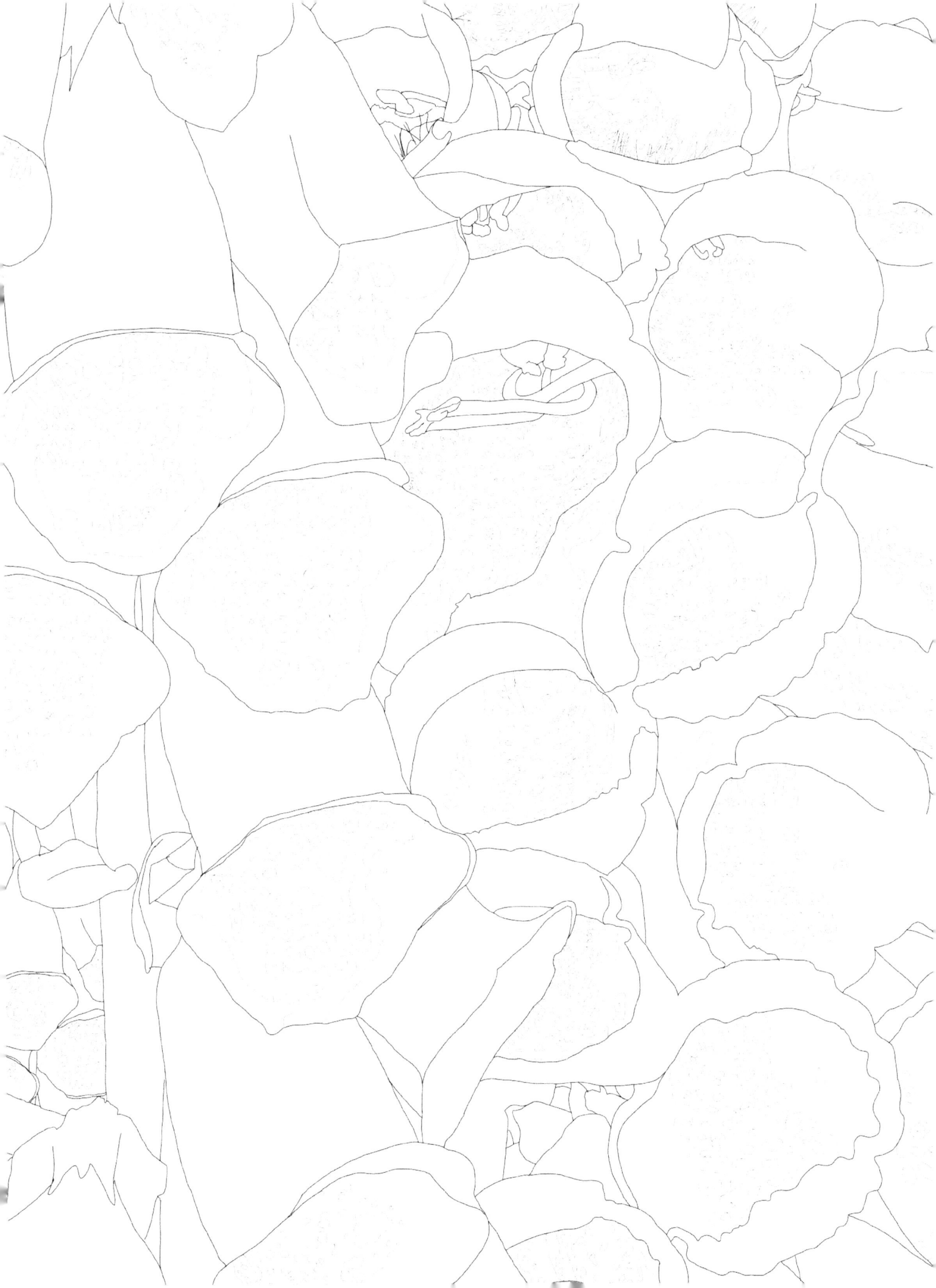

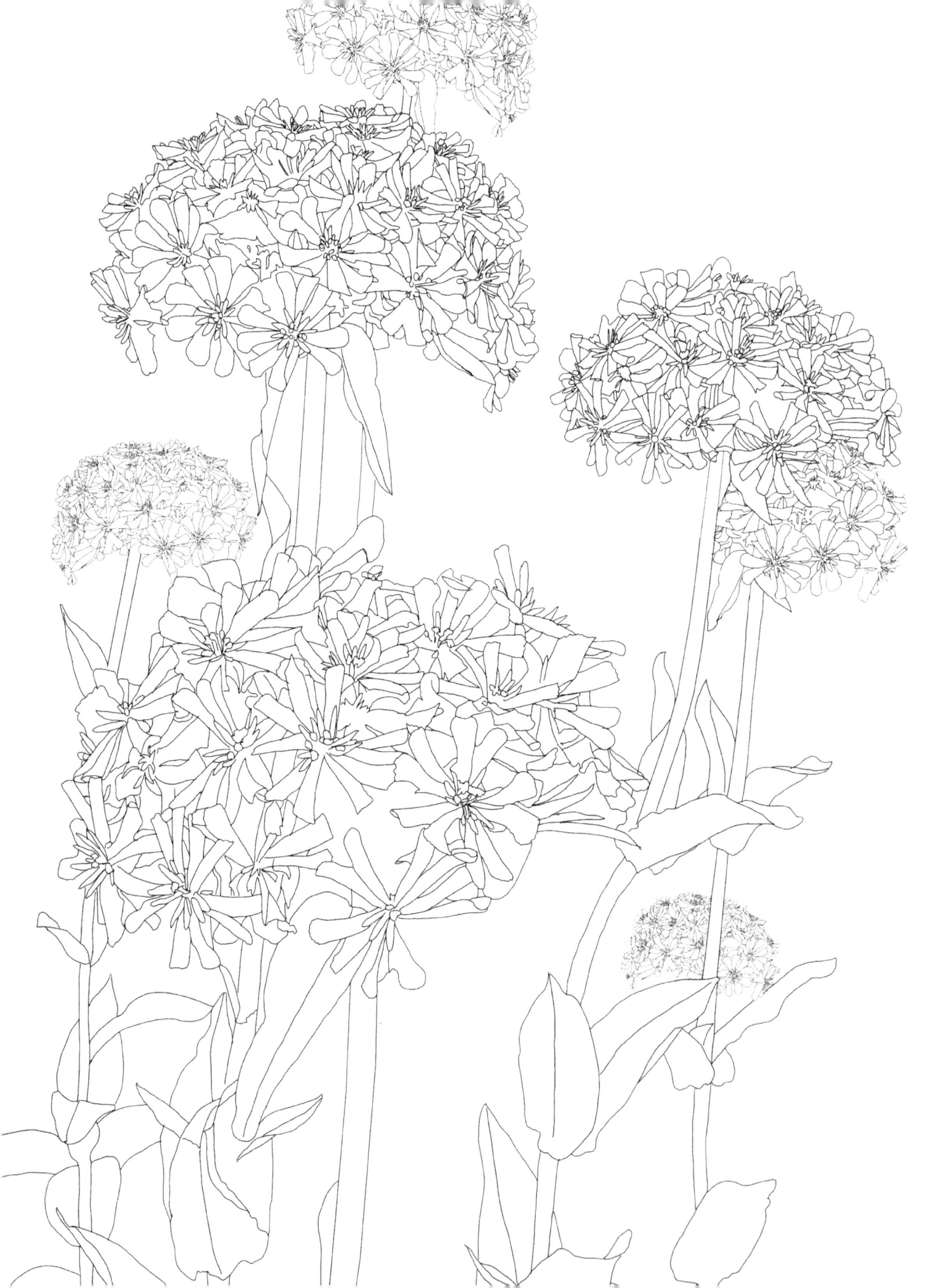

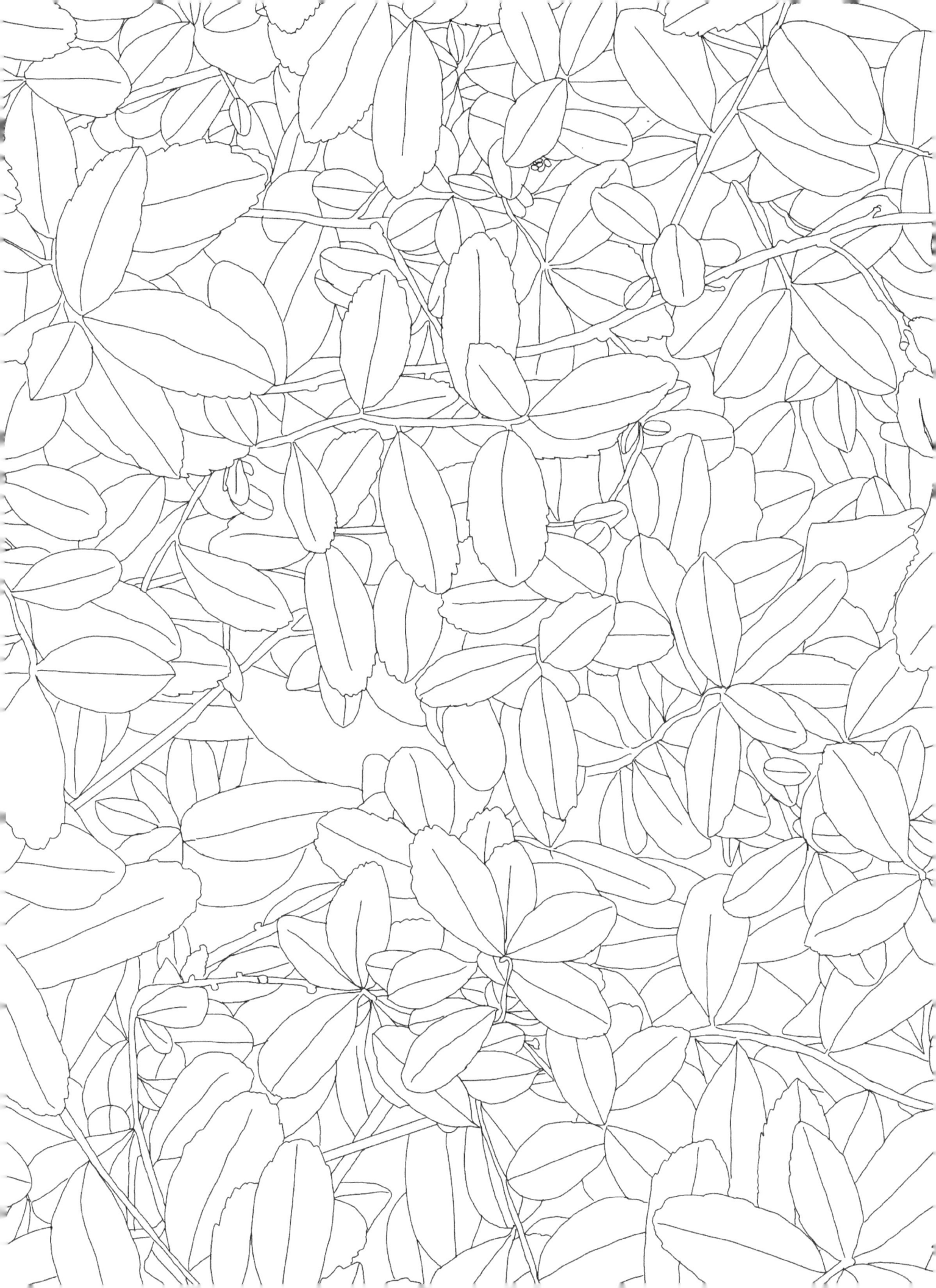

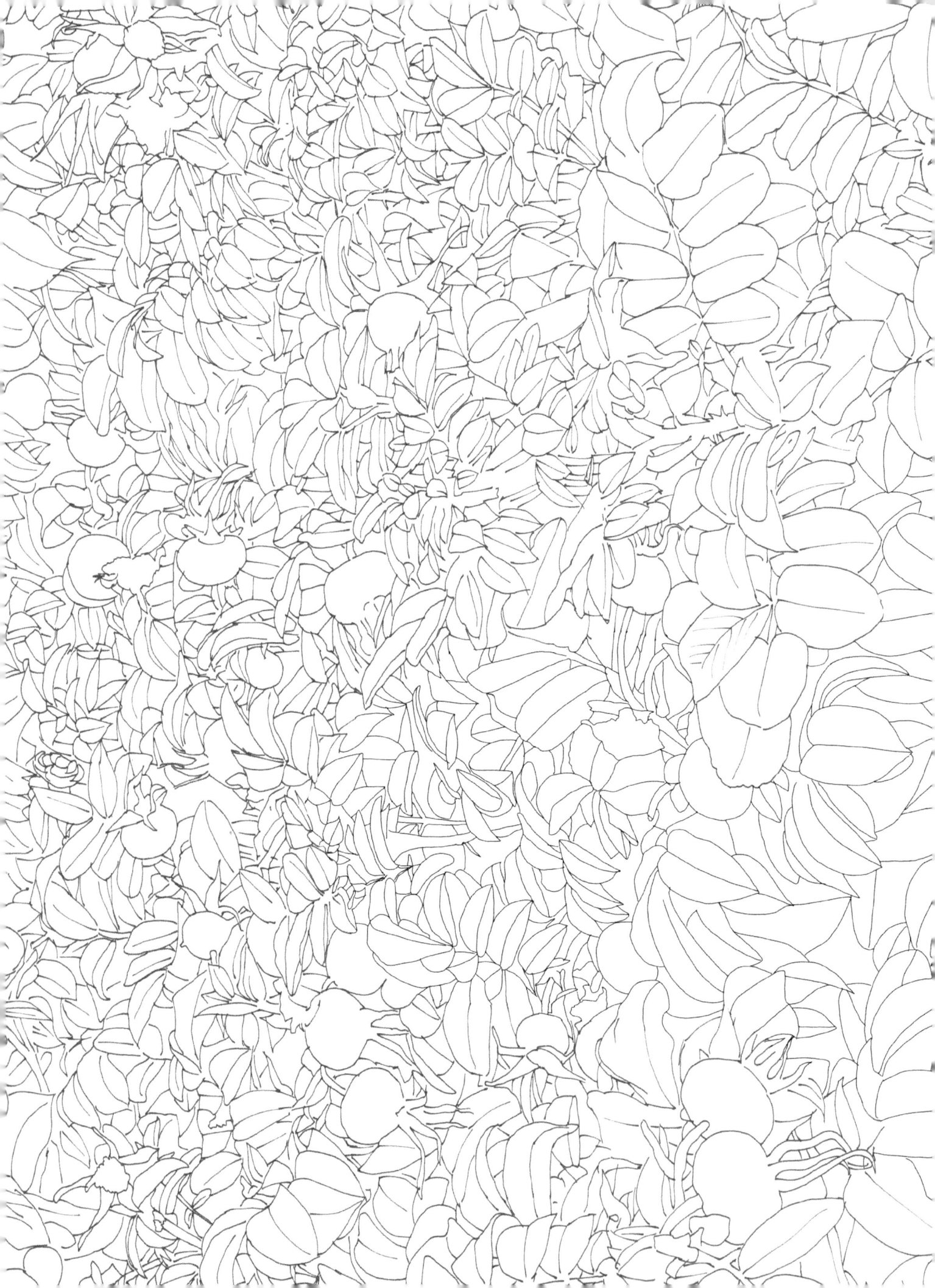

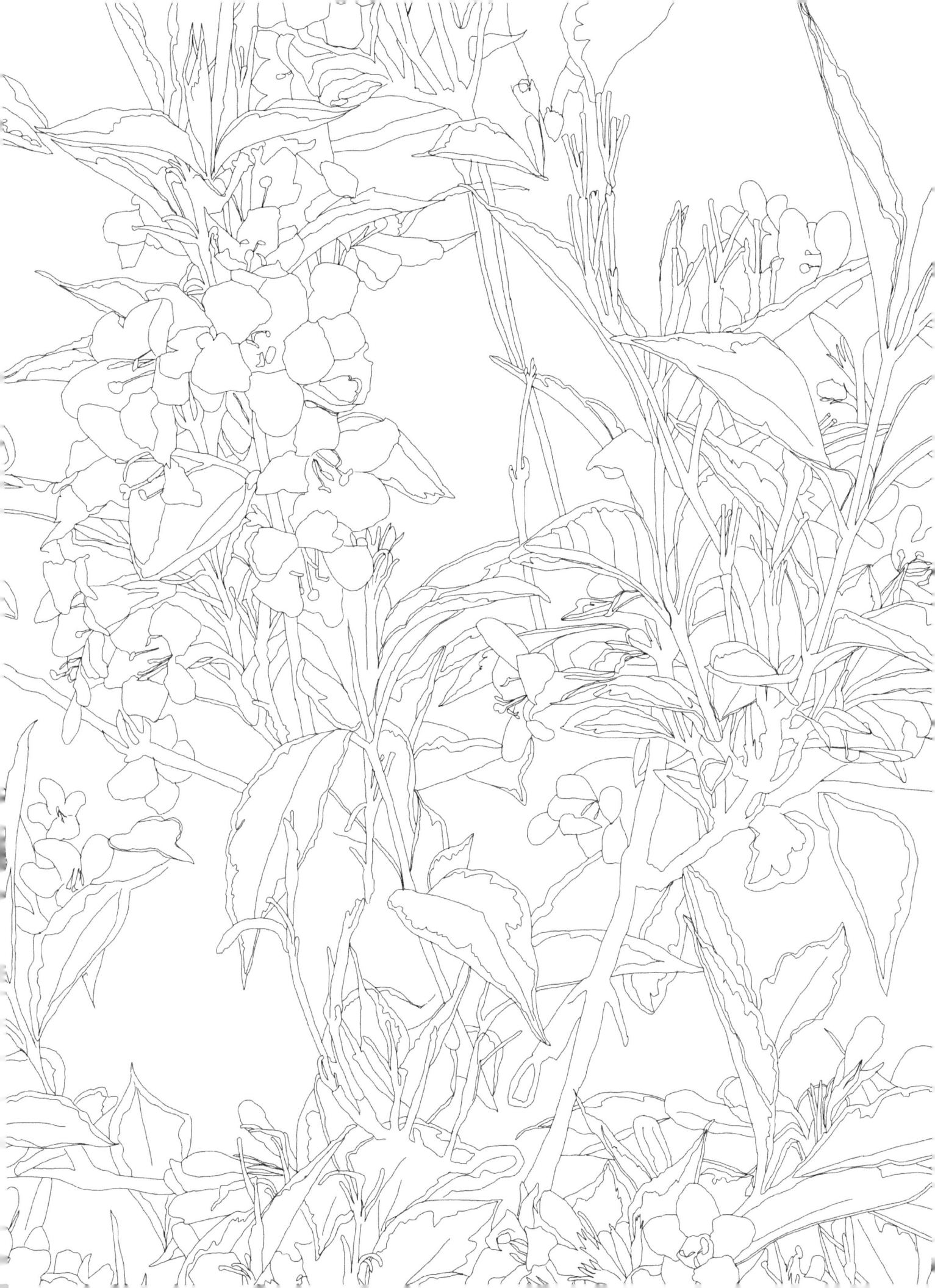

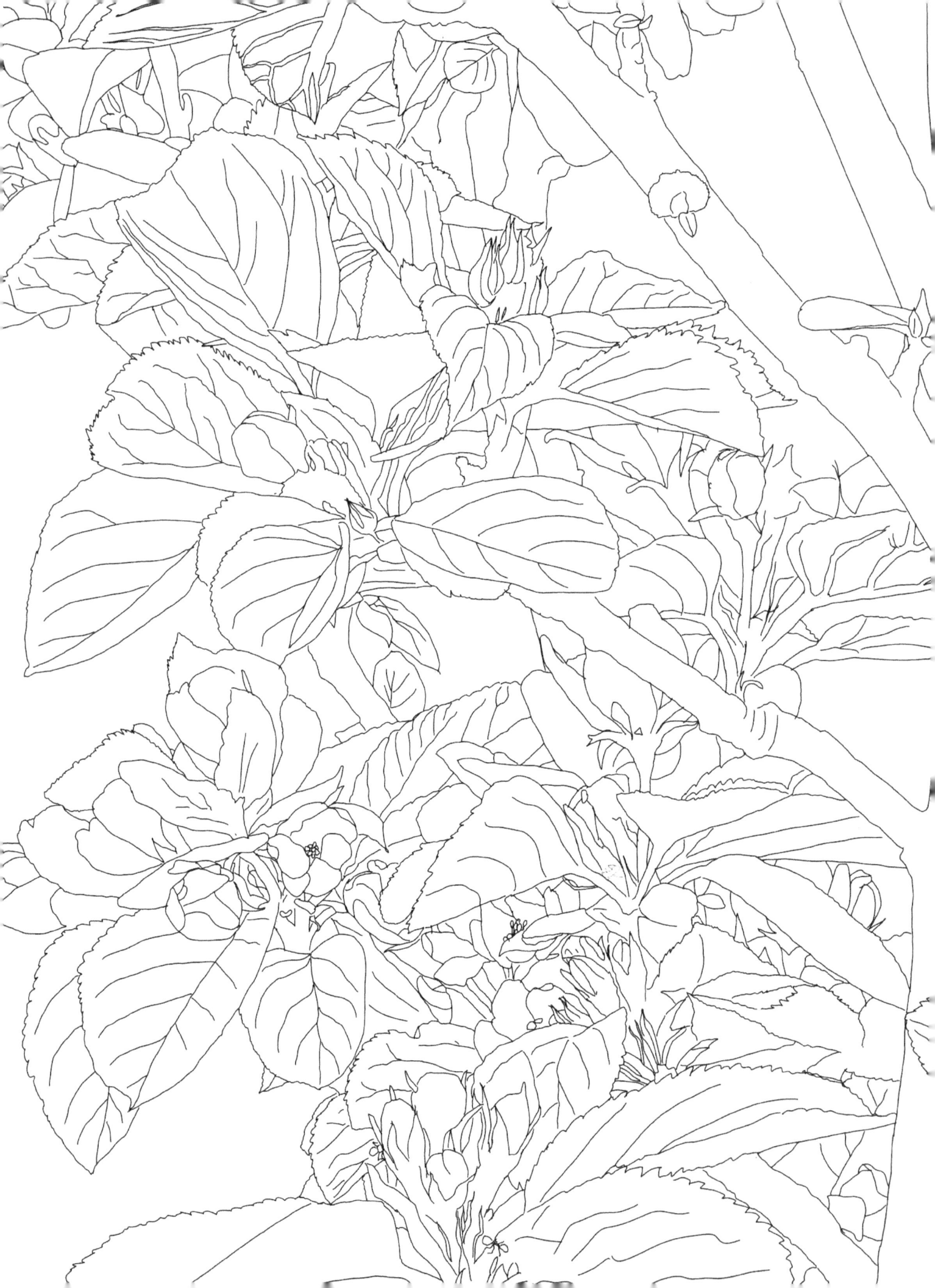

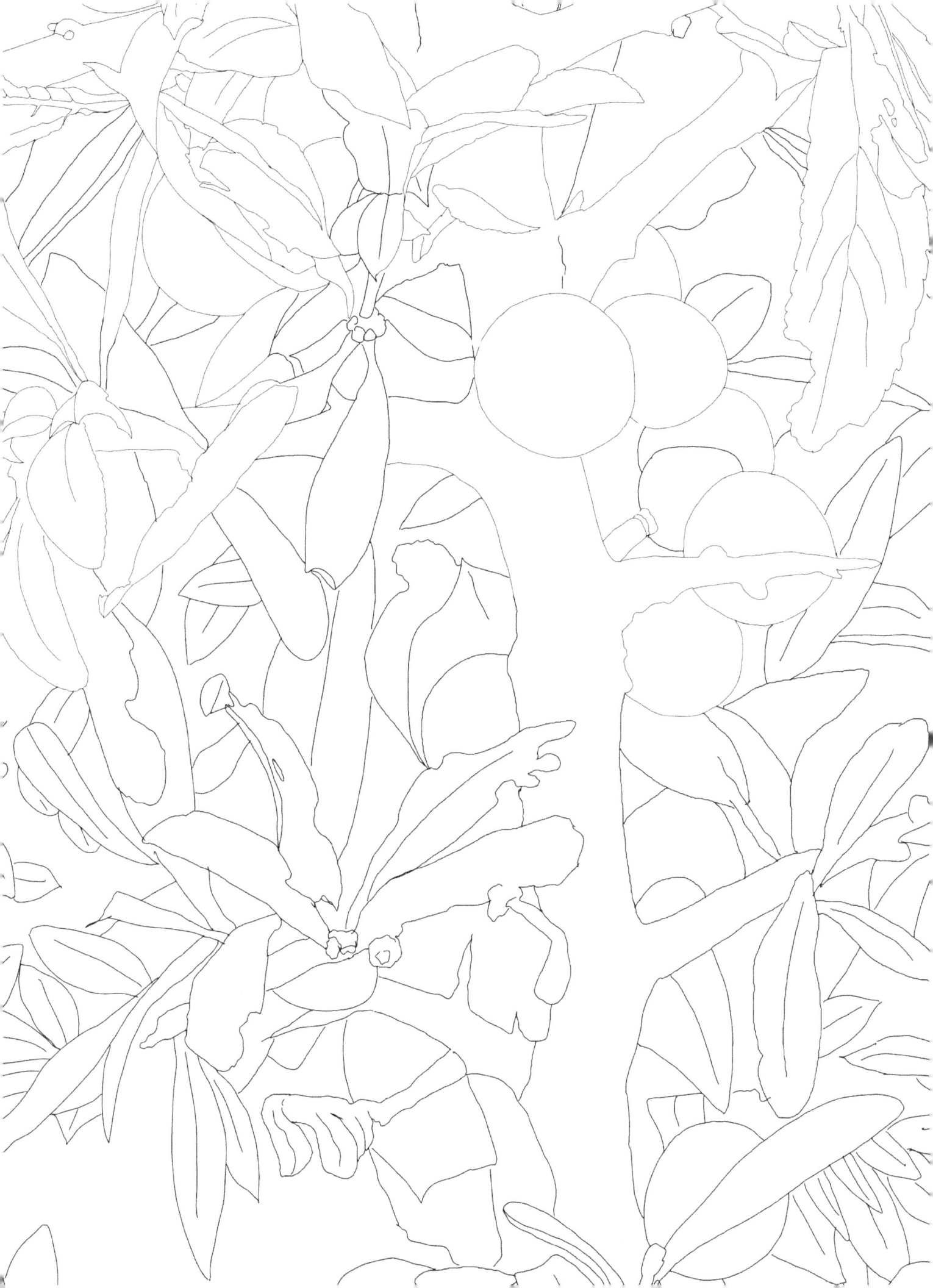

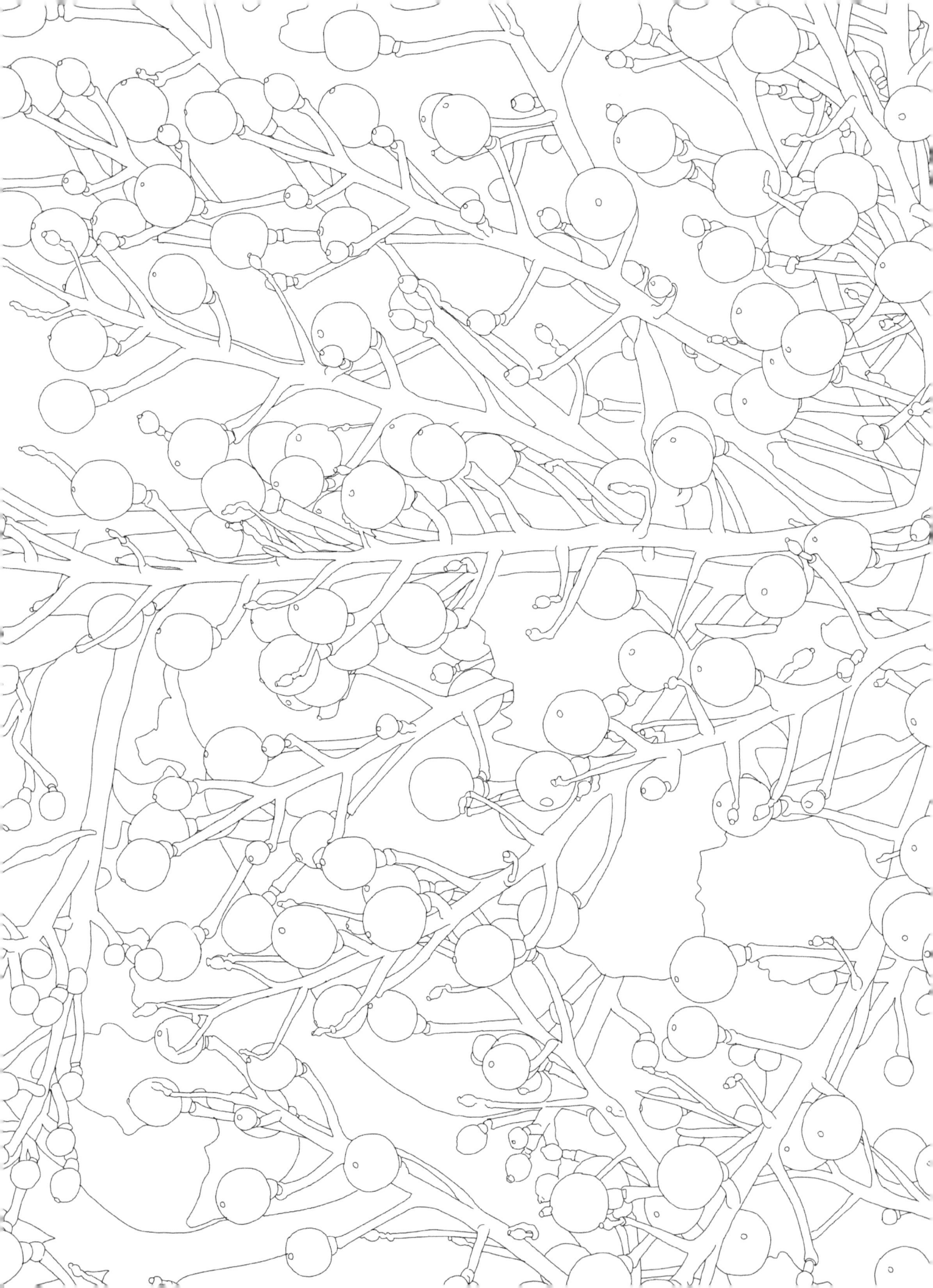

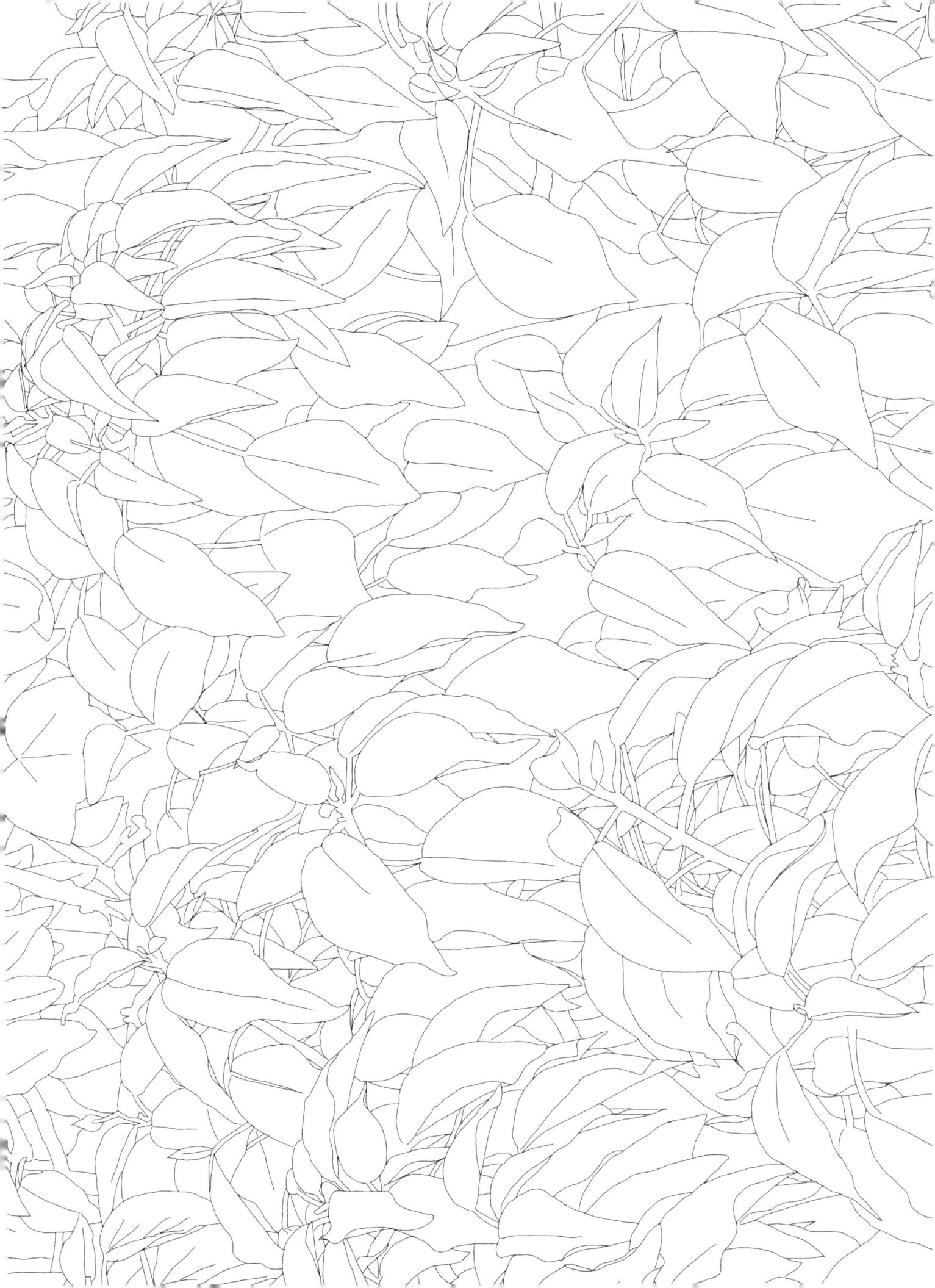

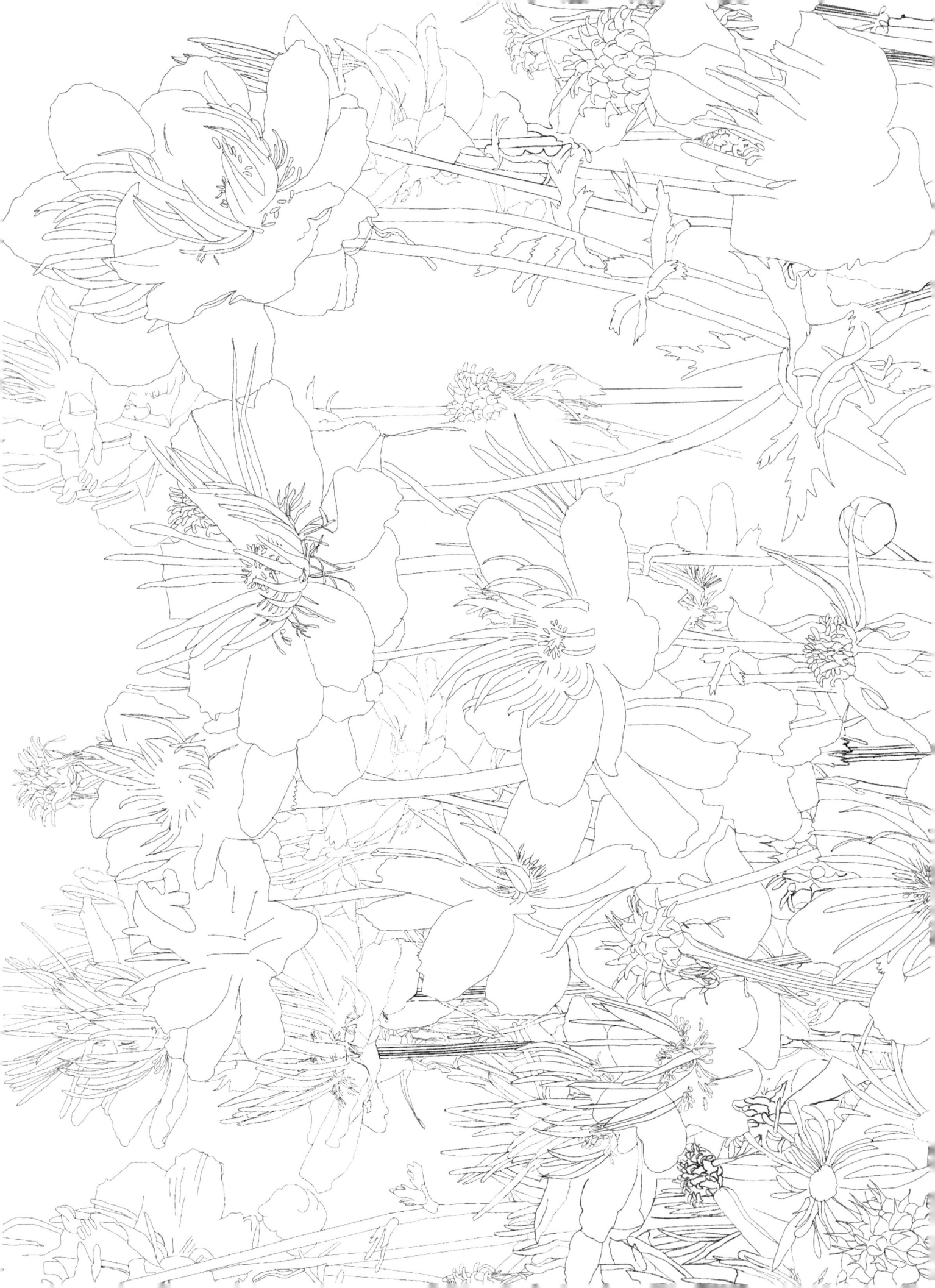

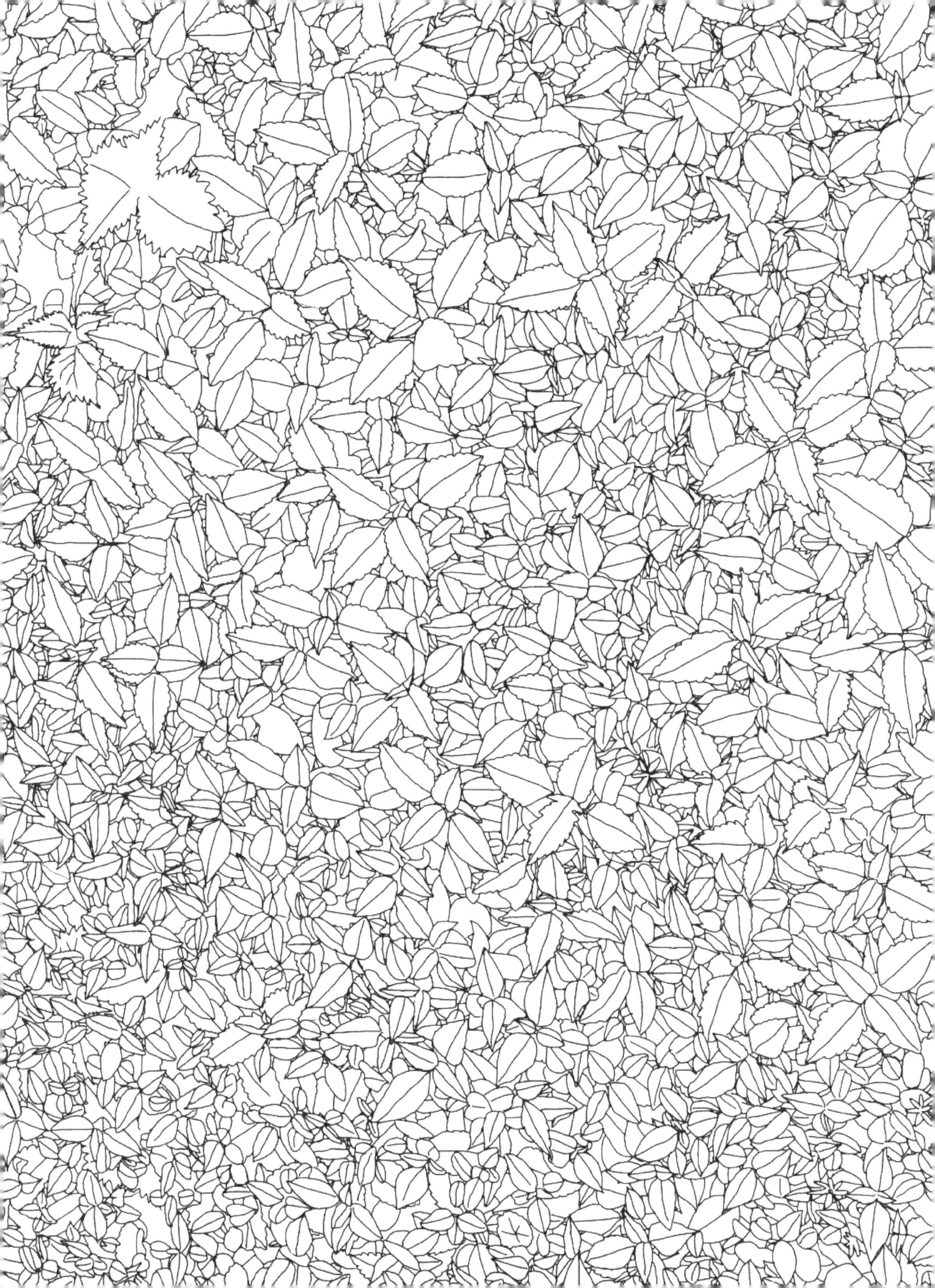

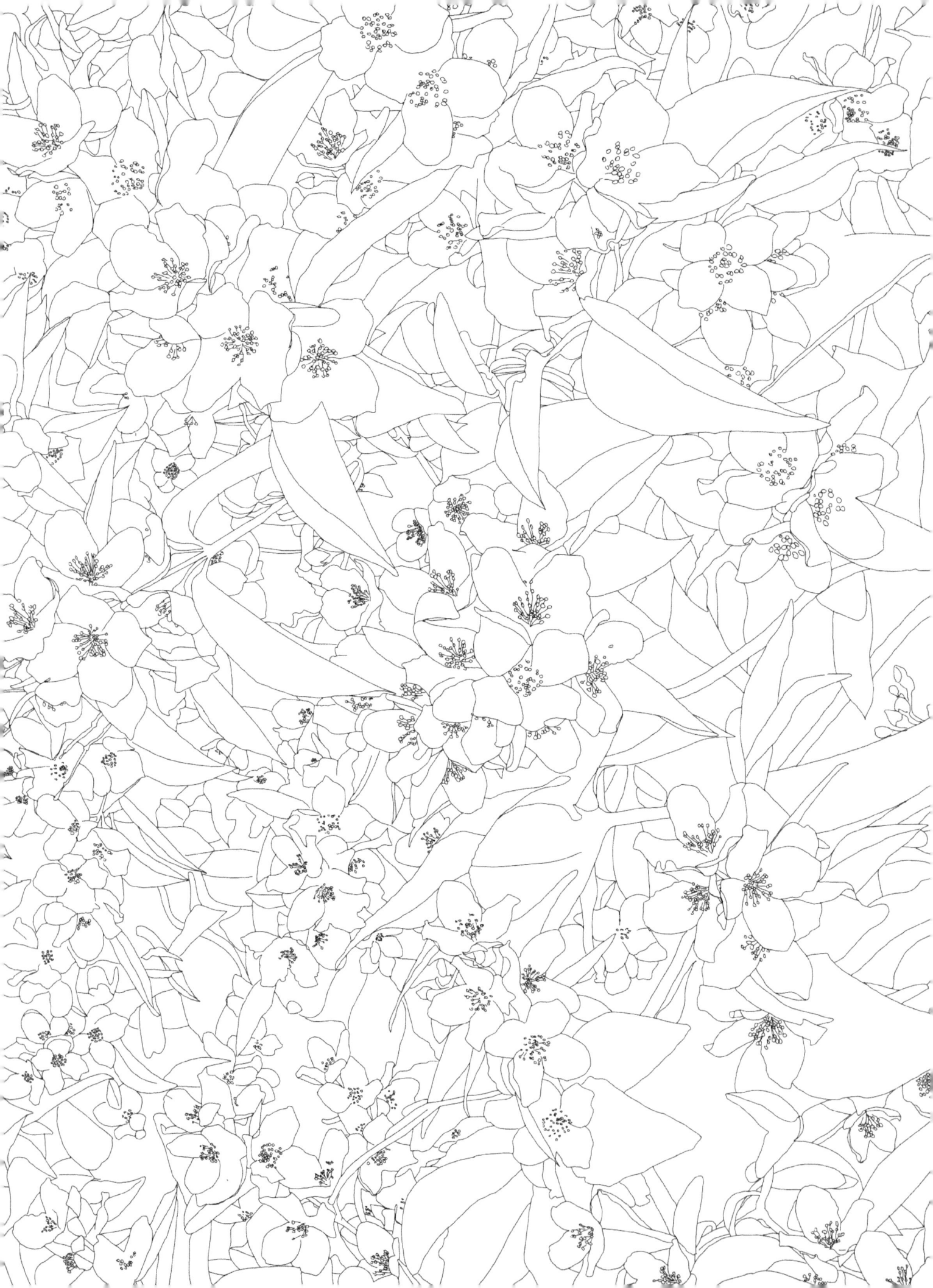

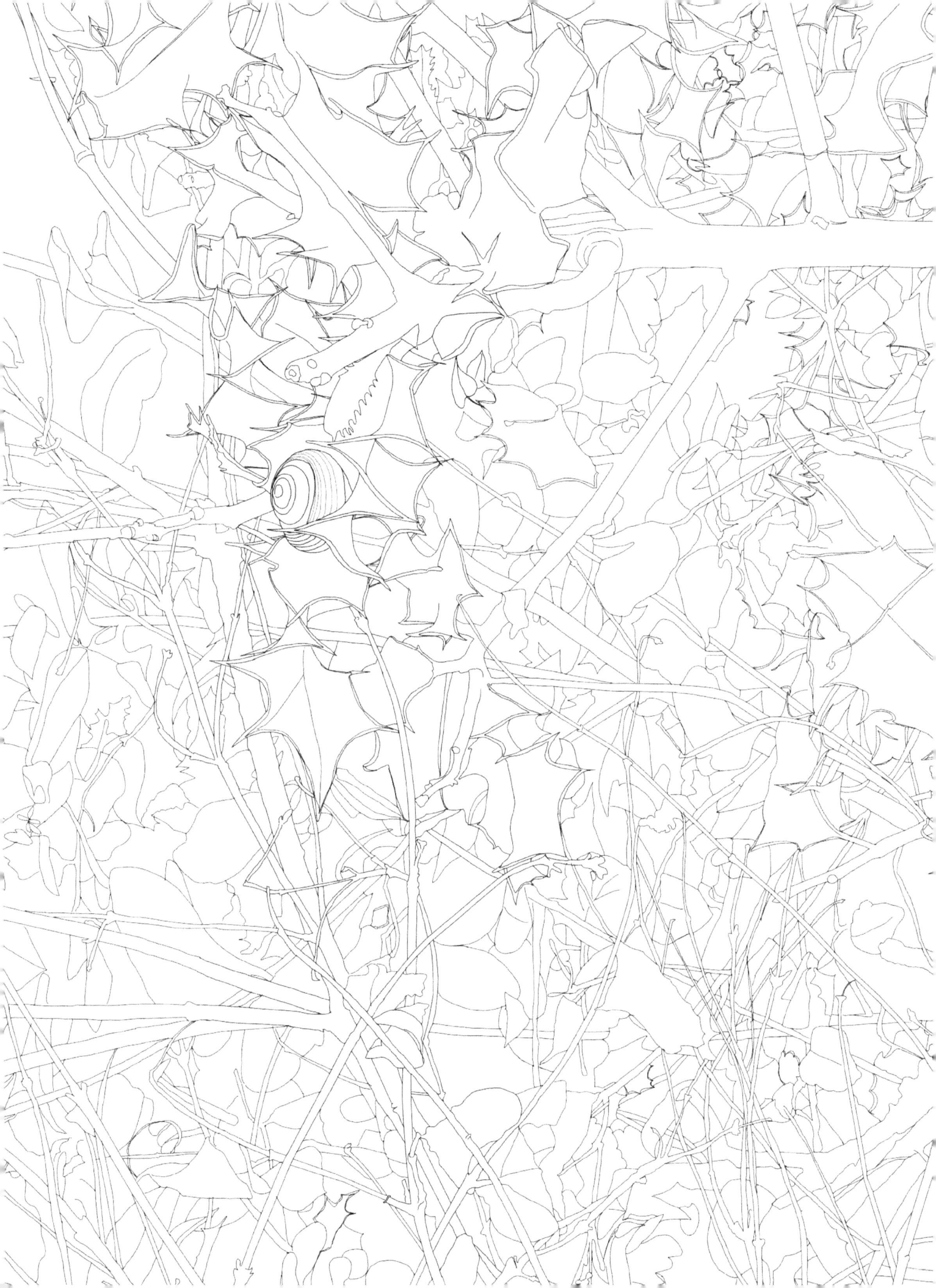

www.ingramcontent.com/pod-product-compliance
Lightning Source LLC
Chambersburg PA
CBHW080643190526
45169CB00009B/3479